# REALITY ORIENTATION FOR THE ELDERLY

# REALITY ORIENTATION FOR THE ELDERLY

## THIRD EDITION

Sylvester Kohut Jr., PhD
Jeraldine J. Kohut, RN, MA, NHA
Joseph J. Fleishman, PhD

MEDICAL ECONOMICS BOOKS
Oradell, New Jersey 07649

**Library of Congress Cataloging in Publication Data**

Kohut, Sylvester, date
  Reality orientation for the elderly

  Includes bibliographies.
    1. Gerontology.   2. Aged—Psychology.   3. Aged
—Care and hygiene.   1. Kohut, Jeraldine Joanne.
II. Fleishman, Joseph J.   III.   Title.   [DNLM:
1. Aged.   2. Cognition disorders—In old age.
WT 150 R288]
HQ1061.K637      1987      305.2'6      86-8308
ISBN 0-87489-436-0

*Design by Douglas Steel*

ISBN 0-87489-436-0

Medical Economics Company Inc.
Oradell, New Jersey 07649

Printed in the United States of America

First Edition      1979
Second Edition    1983
Third Edition     1987

*To Jeremy John Kohut, age 7,*
*and his generation*

# CONTENTS

# PUBLISHER'S NOTES

Sylvester Kohut Jr., PhD, is dean of the College of Education at Kutztown University in Kutztown, Pennsylvania. He has served as a program consultant to numerous hospitals, nursing homes, federal agencies, and educational institutions. He teaches graduate courses on aging education, and conducts seminars on communications dynamics in health care settings including hospices and nursing homes.

Jeraldine Joanne Kohut, RN, MA, NHA, is director of nursing at Westminster Village (Comprehensive Retirement and Nursing Home Complex of Presbyterian Homes, Inc.) in Allentown, Pennsylvania. Formerly, she was an assistant professor of nursing and director of continuing education, School of Nursing, Tennessee Technological University, Cookeville. In collaboration with her husband, she has published widely on the aging process and clinical treatment of the elderly. She was founder and served as executive director of the Hospice of Cookeville, Tennessee, Inc. (United Way). She has served as a nursing home and hospital administrator/consultant and as a nursing educator/geriatric workshop coordinator for numerous institutions and organizations throughout the United States. Her most recent book coauthored with her husband is titled *Hospice: Caring for the Terminally Ill* (Charles C Thomas Publisher, Inc., Springfield, Illinois, 1985).

Joseph J. Fleishman, PhD, is a clinical psychologist in private practice in Bensalem, Pennsylvania. Formerly, he was head clinical psychologist of the Geriatric Psychology Program at Philadelphia State Hospital. While a member of the graduate school faculty at the Gerontology Center of the Institute for the Study of Human Development of The Pennsylvania State University—Capitol Campus in Middletown—he also was a practicing psychologist and gerontologist in Harrisburg, Pennsylvania.

Joseph F. Rodgers, MD, who assisted in the preparation of Chapter 4, is associate dean for Affiliations and Residency Program Coordination with the rank of associate clinical professor of medicine in the Medical School at Thomas Jefferson University, Philadelphia. He has maintained a private practice in internal medicine in Philadelphia for over 25 years. He has delivered scholarly papers on internal medicine research and practices at professional meetings throughout the United States and Europe.

Opless Walker, PharmD, author of Chapters 6 and 7, is a clinical pharmacologist and director of pharmacy services, Cookeville General Hospital, Cookeville, Tennessee. He has conducted workshops and taught courses in pharmacology at Tennessee Technological University, Cookeville, and the University of Tennessee at Knoxville.

"To be seventy years young is sometimes far more cheerful and hopeful than to be forty years old."

—Oliver Wendell Holmes

# INTRODUCTION

Throughout this book we stress the importance of touch. An elderly, confused person whose eyesight, hearing, senses of smell and taste, and physical mobility are failing still has two undiminished capacities—the sense of touch and the sense of self. We can think of no finer introduction than these excerpts from "Touch Me!"* by Hazel James.

## Touch Me!

I am old. The relentless waves of Time have bruised my body; eroded my bones. Skin that was once firm and elastic has shriveled beneath many summers of flaming suns; has become withered from the caress of icy winds of many winters. My steps are now measured and faltering—from my bed to the wheelchair are agonizing miles. I grope blindly for the glass there on the table beside my bed. My hand touches the plastic bowl of plastic flowers and bitterness rises in my heart. Two years ago this past Mother's Day, they sent them. Two long years ago!

Poker-faced, stern, these strangers minister to my needs. Impersonally, they perform those acts necessary for my survival. To them, I'm not a person. Only a number! Number 54 is tendered medication. Number 54 is bathed, dressed, assisted into her wheelchair. Number 54 is brought her tray. And forgotten!

Touch me, so I'll know I'm still a segment of this vitally alive, pulsating world of human beings and not an inanimate number lying here staring daily at a plastic bowl of plastic flowers. As you give me medication, allow your sturdy fingers to press my trembling ones in reassurance. Such an act will bring back sweet memories of other days; of other hands, clinging, clasping baby hands; hands raised in supplication; pleading for love. Your act will unroll the scroll of Time and, once again, I'll feel tiny arms about my neck, squeezing, clinging. Touch me!

*Copyright © *Crisis,* December 1975. Reprinted with permission of the Crisis Publishing Company, Inc.

The endless monologues you hear are not senseless ramblings of disoriented minds. They're the heartcries of forsaken souls begging for remembrance. Only the flicker of an eyelash; the remotest trace of a smile! They're wails of love-starved beings, pleading for a crumb of affection. Look at me!

Touch me! The miracle of physical contact will remove the thick crust of disappointment and disillusionment from a heart battered by unkind years. Number 54 will become a person again; a grateful old woman, alive—and thankful! She'll soar beyond her aches and pains; she'll forget plastic flowers in a plastic bowl, and face her day in peace. Trembling hands will grasp each such moment greedily, never letting go. This old, pain-torn body will be revitalized with hope and purpose for when the heart is happy, the soul sings. You'll see! Just touch me!

# PART 1

# PERSPECTIVES AND INSIGHTS

# 1

## SOCIOLOGY OF AGING

**HISTORICAL ANTECEDENTS**

The American storyteller and humorist Mark Twain once wrote, "There are statistics, more statistics and damn lies." Contrary to Twain's folksy wisdom, statistical data and actuarial records relating to aging population trends and profiles throughout the United States are not only credible but astonishing. The life expectancy of a person born in 1900 was 47 years, and there were only 3 million persons 65 or older in that year. For a person born today, the life expectancy is almost 75 years, and there are now over 26 million senior citizens. In 1900 pneumonia, tuberculosis, and gastroenteritis were the major causes of death. Today, heart disease and cancer are the major causes. Our 26 million elderly represent 12 percent of the total population. Over 2 million live in institutions, and a significant portion of the institutionalized elderly are incapacited by disease and degenerative conditions.

People are living much longer. If a person is already 65 years old, his or her average remaining lifetime is 17 years. If you are a descendant of long-lived ancestors, your genes are coded for an even longer life. It helps to be a woman, too. On the average, American women live 8 years longer than men. Today, life expectancy for men is almost 71 years, while life expectancy for women is amost 79 years. There are approximately

3

four women for every three men in the 65-and-older category. By the year 2030, it's predicted that there will be over 58 million persons aged 65 years or older and that the elderly will constitute 17 percent of the entire population of the United States. In view of these enlightening and somewhat startling statistics, it's no wonder that an awareness of the need to study the aging process and the accompanying problems of the elderly is emerging. Our society's interest in self-preservation is reflected in the currect boom in the fields of gerontolgy and geriatrics.

In most industrialized countries, 65 has become the mandatory age for retirement. Why is age 65 the gateway to the so-called golden years? In the late 19th century, Bismarck, the Prussian dictator, established 65 as the mandatory retirement age, in an attempt to institute social reforms for his subjects. Retirement was then considered a reward from the state for the worker's many years of toil. The regulation made sense, because during that turbulent period in history a person's life expectancy was substantially shorter than it is today; therefore, the actual number of years a worker spent in blissful retirement was few, if any. This made it possible to finance the retirement program without economic strain.

Many industrialized countries with broad technological and Keynesian economic foundations have kept 65 as the mandatory or suggested age of retirement, in the belief that a strong, efficient industrialized society can provide goods and services for all its citizens while "freeing" its elderly to enjoy the better aspects of life. Today, though, it's undeniable that retirement represents a mixed blessing. Retirement may be a reward, but the typical accompanying loss of income and prestige makes one wonder if retirement isn't associated with punishment. In contrast, the less sophisticated agricultural societies utilize their human resources as long as possible. Hence their elderly enjoy lifelong repect and financial security. The 1978 legislation that raised the minimum mandatory retirement age to 70 has influenced the attitudes of unemployed or underemployed younger citizens toward the job-holding elderly.

## THE WORSHIP OF YOUTH

A society is a collection of formally and informally related

4

groups organized for mutual survival. The family, as the primary unit in our society, is responsible for child rearing and the social and moral training of our young. The family transmits traditions and mores from generation to generation, assigns roles and status to its members, and provides a series of rewards, reinforcements, and prohibitions that direct our lives in a manner consistent with society's goals and value systems. Clearly, our society places a premium on youth. Exalting youth, we devote many years to the care, nurturance, and education of our young.

Alvin Toffler, author of *Future Shock*, submits that we live in a transient society where constant, rapid change is commonplace. An unnecessary side effect of this perpetual motion is the well-known generation gap—or gaps—between the young, the middle-aged, and the old. Because the elderly are neither cherished, like the young, nor productive, like the middle-aged, our society makes them feel like obsolete, unwanted burdens.

Each age group has its own balance sheet of credits and debits. Children receive care and nurturance, but they have to depend on others to provide it. Adults gain independence, but they must work hard to sustain it. For many old people, though, the modest credits of leisure and the wisdom that only age and experience can bring are far outweighed by the debits: (1) loss of prestige due to retirement, (2) feelings of aimlessness and uselessness, (3) reduced income, (4) loss of friends who have died, and (5) deteriorating health. The bottom line is self-pity, low self-esteem, and depression.

## THE ELDERLY GO ALONG

Why hasn't this state of affairs led to indignant uprisings? Even the Gray Panther organization hasn't attracted a significant number of the elderly, perhaps because they themselves subscribe to conscious and unconscious prejudices. The most obvious one stems from the Puritan work ethic: "The Devil finds work for idle hands." It's ironic that some of the strongest proponents of the work ethic are likely to be the elderly. This attitude compounds the problems arising from the idleness they face after forced or voluntary retirement.

The elderly encounter other prejudices as well. If they do

seek work, most retired people can't find it; the response from well-meaning employers is usually a loud, clear No. Studies indicate that, except when life is at stake, persons caring for or working with the elderly don't like their jobs and would prefer working with younger people. The negative stereotypes that contribute to the harsh social climate the elderly encounter are typified by three myths: When people grow old, they lose their mental acuity, their independence, and their sexuality.

The fastest growing minority in the United States is the 85-and-over group. What are some of the characteristics of this group today? Born in the Gay Nineties, they have witnessed or participated in the Spanish-American War, World War I, World War II, the Korean conflict, and the Vietnam War. They have seen the introduction of thousands of inventions and medical and scientific wonders. Many of the elderly are immigrants with roots in the Old World. Many, especially the rural poor, have had little formal schooling. Many are proud, patriotic, and religious and tend to believe in spiritual rather than secular or scientific explanations or solutions to problems. Valuing their privacy and what remains of their independence, they are often shy about discussing severe medical problems as well as everyday aches and pains. Like all people, they need love, friendship, understanding, and respect.

---

**Resources**

*Aging* (16mm film). Focuses on the special needs of the elderly and challenges common stereotypes related to the lifestyles of older citizens. Available from James B. Cabell Library, Virginia Commonwealth University, Richmond, VA 23284.

Binstock RH (ed): *Handbook of Aging and the Social Sciences,* ed 2. New York, Van Nostrand Reinhold, 1985.
    Updated edition presenting a wealth of information on concepts, theories, and issues in aging from the perspective of the social sciences.

Busse EW, Maddox GL: *The Duke Longitudinal Studies of Normal Aging 1955-1980: An Overview of History, Design and Findings.* New York, Springer Publishing Co., 1985.
    Two decades of landmark research on the complex process of aging are chronicled in this monograph. Serves as a fine introduction to various studies addressing the biological, behavioral, and social aspects of normal aging.

Lawton MP, Windley PG, Byerts TO: *Aging and the Environment*. New York, Springer Publishing Co., 1982.

Examines knowledge about aging and the environment within the broader context of environment and behavior. Includes information related to the processes of environmental cognition, cognitive mapping, privacy, complexity, and territoriality.

Taylor C: *Growing On: Ideas About Aging*. New York, Van Nostrand Reinhold, 1984.

Collection of provocative ideas on aging drawn from newspapers, letters, diaries, essays, speeches, and poems.

# 2

# PSYCHOLOGICAL ASPECTS OF AGING

As noted in Chapter 1, the elderly have to contend with concrete losses as well as social prejudices. Psychologists use the concept of defense mechanisms to explain how people cope with their problems, including the impositions and aversive qualities of aging. This chapter describes various defense mechanisms and how they may shape personality and temper adjustments during the last part of the life cycle. It also describes the psychological characteristics of the aged. The facts about the general mental status of the elderly contrast markedly with the negative stereotype of mental deterioration.

## COPING OR DEFENSE MECHANISMS

Anna Freud integrated the ideas regarding defense mechanisms. They may be defined as responses to stress and adversity, largely unconscious in nature, that protect someone from awareness of threat or anxiety. Therefore, there are coping and dysfunctional components to defenses. This concept is rooted largely in psychoanalytic thinking, which emphasizes the influences of early experiences and the unconscious. Although others prefer to explain coping processes from a more cognitive viewpoint[1-3] (emphasizing awareness and the rational processes), it's generally acknowledged that defense mechanisms provide a natural explanation of the way people cope.[4,5] Where defenses are viewed as a possible illustration of weaker or less realistic ideas of ongoing events related to life-style, then psychotherapy becomes cognitive and behavioral.[6]

Ten defense mechanisms have been described: repression, denial, projection, intellectualization, rationalization, reaction formation, displacement, fantasy, regression, and identification.

*Repression,* a very basic defense mechanism, means blocking out memories of stressful events. Frequently the memories are of early childhood experiences that threatened psychological security and may include feelings of rejection, anger, sexuality, and dependency.

*Denial* produces glaring distortions of threatening stimuli. A person may deny his or her assaultive or seductive attitudes or behavior, for example. Needless to say, communicating with such a person is very difficult.

*Projection* usually takes two forms; both are partially the result of guilt feelings. One type of projection is illustrated by the example of a woman who's long overdue in returning a borrowed item to a friend. Upon seeing the friend, whose expression is noncommittal, the borrower immediately feels she's being judged unfavorably and may start a long and unnecessary explanation of her tardiness. She has projected her guilt onto her friend's facial expression. In the second type of projection, the person attributes his or her feelings to others without any evidence that they actually have those feelings. The distortions associated with this defense can be striking, and sometimes become so strong as to be obvious delusions that have no connection with objective reality.

*Intellectualization* occurs when a person has developed a rigid (as is the case, in varying degrees, with all defense mechanisms), dispassionate, affectless (emotionless) way of responding to the world because of fear of his or her emotions. Such a person will seem isolated from human feelings.

*Rationalization* is characterized by the use of frequent alibis and blaming of errors or unpleasant occurrences on objects, events, and other people. The rationalizer handles conflict largely by changing his memory of the circumstances that produced it. The event is still recalled, but in an altered way so that it appears "justified." People excuse their errors in a wide variety of ways, not all of which are convincing. In comparison with the other defense mechanisms, though, rationalization is relatively safe. It may even be used as a form of therapy. Recently, teaching people to use rationality and more balanced views in order to cope with anxieties and other dysfunctional affect is a large component of cognitive behavioral therapy.

*Reaction formation* is shown by behavior that's the opposite of what is felt. As with intellectualization, there's a rigid style to this behavior. The person appears to be trying to convince all concerned that the behavior in question reflects his or her true feelings and values. An example might be a person who publicly advocates morality but privately acts immorally or even criminally. "The lady doth protest too much, methinks," from Shakespeare's *Hamlet*, captures the essence of this defense mechanism.

*Displacement* is an important defense and has gone relatively unnoticed. It means directing one's feelings, such as anger, to an object or person that is not the source of the feelings. The relative lack of attention paid to this defense in the literature may reflect its wide use. So many "hang-ups" and sore spots are handed down from one generation to another that students of personality often fail to acknowledge that the process probably occurs through displacement. For instance, a mother who as a child felt rejected by her parents may convey that rejection to her own children. (Sometimes this displacement is accomplished by the mother's continued seeking of her parent's approval; this can place pressures on her children and cause them to resent her and feel rejected.) Linden[7] pointed out the significance of displacement in the conflict between the generations. Often, he says, these conflicts resurface when circumstances associated with old age bring the parents and child together again under one roof. Many of thee feelings have been unresolved since adolescence, and they become surprisingly and frighteningly important when contact between the generations is anticipated or occurs.

In 1975, the National Institute of Mental Health emphasized the importance of being clear about one's attitudes toward aging and the elderly. There's evidence that training along these lines helps staff who work with the aged treat them humanely and prevent institutionalization syndrome, a form of severe alienation that seems to be fostered in many nursing homes (see Chapter 8). The report cites evidence that this training may prevent staff members from displacing their feelings onto nursing-home residents.

*Fantasy* is personified in the dreamer or, more accurately, the daydreamer. Singer[8] has shown the constructive nature of fantasy as an outlet for needs, frustrations, and creativity. The images brought to mind by the fantasy usually reflect the functions it serves. Encouragement of fantasy can frequently relax people and help them express their feelings and ideas. This technique is used by leaders of human relations groups to develop sensitivity and communication among the members,[9] and it's beginning to be used extensively as an aid to working with aged persons.[10]

*Regression* means reverting to childlike mechanisms of handling stress. It's easy to see why many who work with geriatric patients seem most concerned about the childishness of their patients and quite frequently view aging as a regressive process. Regression is more apt to occur during an acute episode of illness or loss than when life is sailing along on an even keel. The patient is probably functioning in a less differentiated, more confused, and more helpless state with regression; the central nervous system is either insulted (acutely or chronically), or psychopathology of a significant type has occurred. Because some sick and infirm elderly contribute to the impression that to age is to regress, it's easy to characterize old people as childlike. But aging is not a disease, and the aged in general do not regress.

*Identification* is usually spoken of within the context of early development. A person who takes on the personality qualities of someone he or she perceives as an agressor identifies with the person: "If you can't beat'em, join'em." In the Freudian scheme, the agressor is typically the parent of the opposite sex. Identification, then, has ironic implications; frequently, a middle-aged person will note with amazement that he or she has the very same parental mannerisms or values that elicited fear, sexual arousal, anger, or feelings of rejection in childhood. The middle-aged offspring may acknowledge these resemblances with pride or anger. Better understanding between the generations can arise as a result of these insights. "The older I grow, the smarter my father gets" sums it up nicely.

Orthodox Freudians take rather strict positions regarding the role of the unconscious and the structure and function of defenses in all individuals.[11-13] It's also acceptable, however, to view defenses as having a cultural nature, being learned in early childhood and contributing to the ways we communicate and relate to others later in life.[14,15] The defenses, which are reinforced by the family—particularly the parents—are more or less adapted to the outside world. This culturally oriented approach makes use of data obtained in experiments on learning and definitely is consistent with and part of the modern didactic and empirical approaches to psychiatry and psychotherapy.[2,16,17] Emphasis here is focused on dysfunction, cognitive contributions to dysfunction, and teaching the patient to rethink conclusions and distortions by teaching how fallacies of all-or-none thinking are operative. Finally, symptom control is mastered by practice and re-evaluation.[18] The aged, with their high incidence of affect disorders (especially depression-related types), are excellent candidates for cognitive (clearly understandable) therapies.

There may be a cause-and-effect relationship between someone's defenses and his or her attitudes and styles of relating to other people and problems. Some elderly people may appear hysterical in their behavior. An older person may act frantic and become extremely fearful. In all likelihood, this is caused by the defense mechanism of denial.

Projection is typically used by a person who sees plots and conspiracies everywhere; such a person is overly suspicious and truly alienated. With the sensory loss and social isolation and loneliness associated with old age today, anyone with a moderate tendency to project is apt to become a nuisance and perhaps even be labeled paranoid.

The "know-it-all" is apt to be using intellectualization. Even though this type of person has a rationale for just about everything, much of what he or she says may be incorrect or highly personal. "All head and no heart," such a person seems

13

cold and afraid of closeness, with emotions that appear to be bottled up and difficult to express.

The "bully" tends to pick on those considered to be inferiors. This person's displaced feelings may be expressed in the form of power or social influence, or even in a physical manner.

"Alibi Ike" has never done anything wrong or made a mistake. Rarely does he admit that he does anything because it feels good; he constructs a rationale that lets him blame something or somebody else.

The "evangelist" uses reaction formation. This person knows the answers and wants to proclaim this knowledge to all the world. In many ways, this is an example of the best defense being a good offense.

"Walter Mitty" is a fantasizer. In his own mind he's accomplished many wonderful deeds; only in reality do hard-to-face deficits exist.

Stanley Cath[19] has demonstrated a concrete, helpful way of thinking about older people and their coping behavior through his ego-ecological system. Loss is the key problem a person faces later in life, and the body, which frequently has lost energy, health, tone—sometimes a limb or organ—is viewed as an important element of individual integrity. Elderly people undergoing psychotherapy complain very often of these bodily losses or mental deficits. Cath places great emphasis on the therapeutic role of the older person's social and physical environment. The therapist and the people with whom the older person has contact make up this psychosocial milieu; it either encourages or discourages constructive coping. Cath tries to help the elderly client compartmentalize or encapsulate the loss and to respond constructively and, later, enthusiastically to the life that remains. Often diagrams depicting the specific physical reasons for a loss will help. In general, positive personal and bodily imagery contributes to positive coping. Cath observed persons diagnosed as having chronic brain syndrome become very lucid as they gained enthusiasm for life by partaking of a healthful psychosocial environment.

It's encouraging to see reversals in some psychiatric attitudes toward the elderly. The clinical gerontology program at New York University[20] reflects some of the changes in the way

14

psychiatrists view older persons. Traditionally, psychiatrists as much as anyone have gone by the adage that you can't teach an old dog new tricks. The idea that, because infancy and early childhood experiences shape adult personality only fairly young people can be helped, is being modified.[21] Cath and others see their elderly clients on a continuing basis, because they acknowledge the capacity to change and the need for help at any time in life.

The relationship between illness and stress is being increasingly explored.[16] For example, psychosomatic illness is caused by stress manifesting itself in bodily reactions. A great deal has been written about mind-over-matter phenomena[22-24] and the effects of stress on health.[25,26] At various geriatric centers, it's becoming more and more common to find the routine practice of yoga, transcendental meditation, and other forms of training the autonomic nervous system (the system that controls involuntary muscle contractions, such as those of the heart and digestive system). Many possibly psychosomatic complaints sometimes associated with old age, such as high blood pressure, headaches, or ulcers, are now often thought to be reactions to stress that can be modified by natural means or by drugs that calm the adrenergic, or excitatory, actions of the autonomic nervous system. A person who appears to be always in a state of panic or anger, or fight versus flight, as Cannon[27] originally stated it, is likely to have psychosomatic complaints. As the years accumulate, the toll on the person's organs becomes more visible. The role of anxiety and its control is most clearly described by Beck in *Anxiety Disorders and Phobias*.[3]

## PSYCHIATRIC PROBLEMS

In addition to showing neurotic behavior, the aged may be psychotic—or they may be well adjusted. While neurotics tend to experience anxiety in their relationships with others and are generally overreactive to life's ups and downs, psychotics tend to lose contact with the stresses of living and can even become dangerous to themselves and/or society. For example, a neurotic may be overly concerned about his or her appearance, but a psychotic person may go out in the snow partly or completely naked. Such a person is so unresponsive to social and physical cues that he creates personal danger.

15

At the time of the 1980 census, approximately 140,000 persons aged 65 or older were confined to psychiatric hospitals, mostly state and county institutions. Another 1,300,000 were housed in nursing homes, and still another 800,000 in old-age residences—a total of about 2,100,000 institutionalized elderly. Among nursing home and old-age home residents, between 60 and 80 percent were diagnosed as moderately to severely mentally disturbed. A study by Pfeiffer (1977) estimated that as many as "15 percent of the elderly population in the United States suffer from significant, substantial, or at least moderate psychopathology."[28]

Busse and Pfeiffer[21] have broken down the distribution of the elderly population requiring general mental care and mental institutional care:

Slightly fewer than 1 percent of persons over age 65 are hospitalized in private or public mental institutions. Of these, roughly half were admitted for psychiatric disorders arising in old age (principally organic brain disease) while the other half are individuals admitted for functional psychosis, principally schizophrenia, who have grown old in the hospital. An additional 3% of old people are residing in nursing homes, homes for the aged, and geriatric or chronic disease hospitals; probably about half of these suffer from significant psychiatric disturbances. Combining these data we can say that between 2 and 3% of old people live in institutions as a result of psychiatric illness. . .

While persons over age 65 make up nearly 30% of patients in public mental hospitals and 11% of those in private psychiatric hospitals, they account for only 2% of the patients seen in psychiatric outpatient clinics. In terms of rates of utilization of outpatient facilities this amounts to only about $\frac{1}{10}$ of 1% of old people receiving outpatient treatment. . .

The composite picture that emerges. . .is that some 5% of old people living in the community are either psychotic or else have severe psychopathology; when persons with neurotic and personality disorders are added this figure increases to some 15%; and when all degrees of psychiatric impairment are included, ranging from mild to severe, then 25% to nearly 60% of the aged are affected.

It's clear that a large percentage of the elderly experience moderate and sometimes severe emotional problems without seeking or obtaining professional help. To a certain extent, this may be due to lack of acceptance of the value of modern psychiatry—a specialty that may be no older than they are. Many may not understand psychiatric approaches to personal and intangible concerns. Likewise, as mentioned earlier, may psychiatrists are still biased against the elderly. This bias ignores the accomplishments and strengths of the present generation of survivors.[29] More concretely, psychiatric care is prohibitively expensive for a person on a fixed, limited income. Medicare (medical insurance for the aged) pays for only 190 days total *lifetime* psychiatric hospitalization and for psychiatric outpatient treatment only $250 per year after the patient pays the first $75. The inadequacy of this support is clear. For all these reasons, today's elders too often don't receive attention for their emotional problems until they get severe enough to require commitment to a public mental institution. Of promise are the testing procedures conducted by psychologists and paid for by Medicare. Furthermore, the payment ceiling for psychiatric visits are increased when home and nursing home visits are made. Hence, a fairly effective cooperative method for treating the elderly with significant psychiatric problems is present as primary physicians, psychologists, and psychiatrists pool their talents in treating the patients outside of a psychiatric hospital.

There is a strong need for outpatient programs and intermediate-care facilities that deal effectively with emotional and adaptive problems not drastic enough to require long-term commitment to a mental institution.[21] The problems of depression,[7,20] regression, and psychotic reactions,[7,19] and social breakdown syndrome (a form of severe alienation among the elderly in society)[7] are beginning to be studied and treated in their early stages at selected locations. The outpatient center of the Jefferson Medical Center in Philadelphia treats these problems under Dr. Maurice Linden's direction. New York University's Postgraduate Center offers a clinical gerontology program that treats depression and other emotional problems of the aged and trains competent workers to help these people.

Harrisburg (Pa.) Hospital houses a geriatric center that pays particular attention to the complex of behavior in the elderly that results from loss of health, emotional problems, social isolation, and confusion. At present, many nursing homes and families are frustrated in their ability to cope with such individuals and are sometimes forced to commit them to state mental institutions or overuse psychotropic (mind-controlling) drugs. Intermediate facilities such as geriatric centers are intended to allow aged persons to return to a more even emotional keel and conduct their lives with dignity.

## THE NORMALLY ADJUSTED

Normally adjusted individuals are able to face some very grim realities as long as the circumstances of their lives allow them to remain outgoing and communicative. For many such people, retirement means the opportunity to do the things they've never had time for. It's important to remember that even a well-adjusted individual will use his or her unique, proven coping style to deal with the losses that will inevitably occur in old age. A certain amount of loneliness and depression is therefore par for the course in normal aging.[21,29,30] Unfortunately, not enough is known (or said) about normal coping processes; instead psychology has focused on the negative and attention-getting aspects of behavior. One thing is certain, however: The ability to share feelings is a positive sign of mental health. Abscence of the more dysfunctional symptoms is another positive sign.

## THE PSYCHOLOGICAL ASPECTS OF AGING

Birren[31] edited a handbook on aging that reported a large number of studies on the elderly showing deficits in sensory processes, psychomotor performance, reaction time, reflex time, and so on, compared with control groups. Only more recently have the extent and meaning of these deficits been examined.[30]

True, there are sensory-sensitive and sensory-motor decre-
ments, but they're usually tiny—for instance, $\frac{1}{1000}$ of a second
in reaction time. While a millisecond may be important to a bat-
ter facing the New York Yankee's Dave Righetti's fast ball or an
athlete running the 100-yard dash, this quickness is not required for most of us. Fleishman and Dusek[32] have shown that
time pressures create extra stress that rattles older people, so
it's generally advisable to be patient with them—or anyone—if
you want them to do their best.

Since Biblical times, much has been written about the cognitive stability of older persons, and research[30,33] has shown
that the elderly are as competent as anybody in making use of
long-term memory to arrive at decisions. The fact that they may
take a little longer is offset by the greater number of memories
they've stored up. Having a wealth of experience to draw on
contributes a perspective that a younger person simply can't
supply. For practical purposes, therefore, the elderly can do
just about anything as well as their younger counterparts, as
long as they're given the time.

## SOME GENERAL PERSONALITY QUALITIES

Some general rules of thumb have been suggested concerning
the personalities of the old. Old age is usually expected to inten-
sify personal quirks and weaknesses.[29] Taylor has pointed out
that fantasizing on past accomplishments is normal and
shouldn't be discouraged. More passive social interaction is
also normal;[30] it isn't unusual to find an old person deriving
pleasure from simply observing rather than actually taking part
in group activities.

When analyzed closely, many of the so-called symptoms of
aging are due to the roles imposed on the elderly in the late 20th
century. Quite often, these symptoms result from social and
physical deprivation as well as role expectations. Many old people probably "act their age" simply because they feel expected
to do so. It's as if they were saying, "OK, if you need to see me
act this way, I can use it to my benefit."

---

**References**
1. Raimy V: *Misunderstandings of the Self: Cognitive Psychotherapy and the Mis-*

*conception Hypothesis.* San Francisco, Jossey-Bass, 1975.

2. Beck AT, Rush JA, Shaw B: *Cognitive Therapy of Depression.* New York, The Guilford Press, 1979.

3. Beck AT, Emery G, Greenberg R: *Anxiety Disorders and Phobias: A Cognitive Perspective.* New York, Basic Books, Inc, 1985.

4. Coelho A, Hamburg D, Adams C: *Coping and Adaptation.* New York, Basic Books, Inc, 1974.

5. Greenacre P: *Emotional Growth: Psychoanalytic Studies of the Gifted and a Great Variety of Other Individuals.* New York, International Universities Press, 1971.

6. BecK AT: *Cognitive Therapy and Emotional Disorders.* New York, International Universities Press, 1976.

7. Linden M: Paper presented at Continuing Education Conference on Society and the Aging, Harrisburg Area Community College, Harrisburg, PA, 1974.

8. Singer J: *The Inner World of Daydreaming.* New York, Harper and Row, 1976.

9. Pfeiffer JW, Jones JE (eds): *The 1974 Annual Handbook for Group Facilitators.* La Jolla, CA, University Associates, 1974.

10. Weiner I (ed): *Clinical Methods in Psychology.* New York, Wiley-Interscience, 1976.

11. Blau D, Berezin M: Neuroses and character disorders, in Howells JC (ed): *Modern Perspectives in the Psychiatry of Old Age.* New York, Bruner-Mazel, 1975.

12. Goldfarb A: Institutional care for the aged, in Busse E, Pfeiffer E (eds): *Behavior and Adaptation in Late Life,* ed 2. Boston, Little, Brown, 1977.

13. Berezin M: Paper presented at Continuing Education Conference on Psychodynamics of Aging at New York University Postgraduate Center for Mental Health, New York, 1976.

14. Horney K: *The Neurotic Personality of Our Time.* New York, Norton, 1937.

15. Dollard J, Miller N: *Personality and Psychotherapy.* New York, McGraw-Hill, 1950.

16. Meichenbaum D: *Cognitive Behavior Modification: An Integrative Approach.* New York, Plenum, 1979.

17. Lazarus AA: *In the Mind's Eye.* New York, Rawson, 1978.

18. Burns DD: *Feeling Good: The New Mood Therapy.* New York, The New American Library, 1980.

19. Cath S: Paper presented at Continuing Education Conference on Psychodynamics of Aging at New York University Postgraduate Center for Mental Health, New York, 1976.

20. Blum J: Paper presented at Continuing Education Conference on Psychodynamics of Aging at New York University Postgraduate Center for Men-

tal Health, New York, 1976.

21. Busse E, Pfeiffer E (eds): *Behavior and Adaptation in Late Life*, ed 2. Boston, Little, Brown, 1977.

22. Whittaker J, Fleishman J: Biological foundations of psychology: Behavior and states of awareness, in *Introduction to Psychology*, ed 3. Philadelphia, Saunders, 1976.

23. Nolen WA: *Healing: A Doctor in Search of a Miracle*. New York, Random House, 1975.

24. Brown B: *New Mind, New Body*. New York, Harper and Row, 1975.

25. Stieglitz E: The personal challenge of aging: Biological changes and maintenance of health, in Tibbitts C, Donahue W (eds): *Aging in Today's Society*. Englewood Cliffs, NJ, Prentice-Hall, 1960.

26. Selye H: *Stress Without Distress*. Philadelphia, Lippincott, 1974.

27. Cannon WB: *The Wisdom of the Body*. New York, Norton, 1932.

28. Pfeiffer E: Psychopathology and social pathology, in Birren JE, Schaie KW (eds): *Handbook of the Psychology of the Aging*. New York, Van Nostrand Reinhold, 1977.

29. Curtin S: *Nobody Ever Died of Old Age*. Boston, Little, Brown, 1972.

30. Taylor C: Paper presented at Continuing Education Conference on Society and the Aging, Harrisburg Area Community College, Harrisburg, PA, 1974.

31. Birren JE (ed): *Handbook of Aging and the Individual*. Chicago, University of Chicago Press, 1960.

32. Fleishman J, Dusek ER: The equivalence of alternate forms of six psychometric measures during repeated testing. *Journal of Applied Psychology* 1972; 56:186.

33. Eisdorfer C: Intellectual and cognitive changes in the aged, in Busse E, Pfeiffer E (eds): *Behavior and Adaptation in Late Life*. Boston, Little, Brown, 1969.

**Resources**

Beck AT: *Cognitive Therapy and the Emotional Disorders*. New York, International al Universities Press, 1976.

Birren JE, (ed): *Handbook of the Psychology of Aging*, ed 2. New York, Van Nostrand Reinhold, 1985.

Breslau L, Haug M, (eds): *Depression and Aging*. New York, Springer Publishing Co., 1983.
    Eclectic approach to the dilemmas and disputes over the definition of depression in the elderly; its causes, and effective treatments.

Butler RN, Gleason HP: *Productive Aging*. New York, Springer Publishing Co., 1985.
    A collection of essays by well-known authors and researchers looking

at a somewhat underdeveloped topic—productivity in old age.

Craik F, Trehub S, (eds): *Aging and Cognitive Processes.* New York, Plenum, 1982.

Lazarus RS, Folkman S: *Stress, Appraisal, and Coping.* New York, Springer Publishing Co., 1984.
    An integrative analysis of the subject highlighting the concepts of cognitive appraisal and coping.

*Peege* (16 mm film). A "must" film for any person who deals with an institutionalized, confused, elderly person. A 28 minute color film produced in 1973, it is available from Phoenix Films, 743 Alexander Road, Princeton, NJ 08540.

Teri L, Lewisohn PM: *Geropsychological Assessment and Treatment: Selected Topics.* New York, Springer Publishing Co., 1985.
    A comprehensive review of information on the assessment and treatment of the psychological problems encountered by older adults.

Whitehead T: *Psychiatric Disorders in Old Age: A Handbook for the Clinical Team,* ed 2. New York, Springer Publishing Co., 1979.

# 3

# THE STEREOTYPE OF DEPENDENCE

One of the common assumptions about aging is that it brings excessive dependence on others. However, the evidence concerning three reasonably good indicators of dependence—reliance on others for living arrangements, health care, and finances—simply doesn't support this idea.

## LIVING ARRANGEMENTS

According to Manley,[1] 75 percent of the elderly own their own homes. Typically, these homes are located in urban areas that have been deserted by younger, white, middle-class families who have moved to the suburbs. These homes are generally strongly built[1] and have served well for raising children. Most of them are fully paid for and, therefore, are relatively cheap to own. This is important for someone on a limited fixed income. The elderly are deeply rooted in their homes and communities. They know their way around; their neighbors and surroundings are familiar. Many of their friendships are longlasting and provide a source of mutual help.

Practical problems do arise, however, in maintaining independence—for example, lack of transportation and difficulty in getting up and down stairs. Transportation for the elderly has become an important social issue. Many state programs for the elderly are designed to overcome some of these physical obstacles and make the difference between living at home and entering an institution. Certain state offices of the aging, for instance, operate programs to help meet practical needs arising from incapacities that frequently occur after age 75 and require some form of home care. Strong arguments can be made that these programs allow the elderly to remain in their own homes. This can be especially important to those who have gardens where they can save money by growing food, get exercise, and satisfy their desire for beauty.

Shanas[2] has presented some informative data on how often older persons communicate with their families. Approximately 80 percent of the elderly who were interviewed in that study lived within a half-hour's distance from at least one of their children. Two thirds had seen a child within 24 hours. To a great extent, therefore, the popular image of the isolated elderly is unrealistic. These people are neither isolated nor dependent. It appears that relatives do satisfy many of the social, financial, and affectional needs of the elderly and help them maintain their independence. This idea is definitely supported by data describing the family ties of the institutionalized elderly (see Chapter 8), which suggest that a large percentage are without family.[3]

## HEALTH—MYTHS AGAIN

As mentioned earlier, it's often the picture of the sick or feeble geriatric patient that causes our misconceptions about aging. The elderly are much healthier, on the whole, than we may think. Estes[4] reported a comprehensive summary of the distribution of illness among the aged. The aged definitely suffer more chronic conditions such as high blood pressure, diabetes, and heart disease, but have fewer acute illnesses than younger people, although acute illnesses, when they do occur, are likely to be more severe. Not all chronic illnesses, in fact, depend on age. For example, many younger people have high blood pressure; autopsies of young soldiers during the Vietnam War revealed a high incidence of hardening of the arteries.

The aged also spend less time in bed due to illness than we may think. In 1980 the average hospital stay for persons 65 and over was 10.8 days, compared with 7.2 days for the population as a whole.[5]

Today there are debates concerning new regulations that shorten the hospital stay of the very ill because of new third party payment rules. Reimbursement to hospitals is based upon the *illness*, *not* the total number of *days spent in the hospital*. Thus, statistics related to the "average" hospital stay can be misleading. Hospitals are being discouraged from allowing patients (often the elderly) to remain in the hospital. Financial controls that limit hospital stays do not necessarily mean better health care for the elderly.

Stieglitz[6] has an interesting theory on the loss of reserve energy that seems to occur with the wear and tear of age and stress. This reserve—or second wind—is what we draw on when we get tired. Lack of it seems to be what people allude to when they say they're feeling older. Actually, it's stress and daily wear and tear,[6,7] rather than age, that impairs the body's homeostatic (self-stabilizing) processes. Nonetheless, we blame age for the slowness we sometimes feel. There are many ways to minimize the loss of reserve energy: Regular exercise, good nutrition, meditation, and avoidance of smoking all improve circulation of the blood and contribute to general homeostasis.

## FINANCES

In a capitalist country, loss of income means loss of social status and presages loss of independence. Therefore, loss of income is a very strong and realistic source of fear.

The four main sources of income for the aged, in addition to assistance from children, are Social Security, pensions, salaries and wages, and public welfare programs.[8] The true picture doesn't seem as gloomy as sometimes described. More than 18 percent of elderly men and nearly 8 percent of elderly women are still working, even though they may hold part- instead of full-time jobs.[5] There has also been a large increase in the number and value of pensions available to retirees during the last 30 years.

In March 1980, the mean income of families headed by persons aged 65 or over was $14,727, compared with a mean income for all United States families of $22,376. Only 9.1 percent of families headed by persons 65 or over were below the poverty level, the same percentage as for all United States fam-

25

ilies. So it's clear that insofar as actual poverty is concerned, the elderly are no worse off than the population in general.[5]

There are savings. For most elderly people who own their own homes, there are no rent or mortgage payments. With retirement comes extra time for do-it-yourself projects that can provide goods and services that were formally purchased. These are often swapped informally with friends and neighbors.

The elderly, though sometimes in straitened circumstances, are remarkably proud and independent. The stereotype of financial dependence in old age simply doesn't hold water.

---

### References

1. Manley HN: Statistics cited in: Busse E, Pfeiffer E (eds): *Behavior and Adaptation in Late Life*. Boston, Little, Brown, 1969.

2. Shanas E: Living arrangements and housing of old people, in Busse E, Pfeiffer E (eds): *Behavior and Adaptation in Late Life*. Boston, Little, Brown, 1969.

3. Goldfarb A: Institutional care for the aged, in Busse E, Pfeiffer E (eds): *Behavior and Adaptation in Late Life*. Boston, Little, Brown, 1969.

4. Estes H, Jr.: Health experience in the elderly, in Busse E, Pfeiffer E (eds): *Behavior and Adaptation in Late Life*. Boston, Little, Brown, 1969.

5. *Statistical Abstract of the United States: 1981*, 102nd ed. U.S. Bureau of the Census. Washington, D.C., U.S. Government Printing Office, 1981.

6. Stieglitz E: The personal challenge of aging: Biological changes and maintenance of health, in Tibbitts C, Donahue W (eds): *Aging in Today's Society*. Englewood Cliffs, NJ, Prentice-Hall, 1960.

7. Selye H: *Stress Without Distress*. Philadelphia, Lippincott, 1974.

8. Rich T, Gilmore A: *Basic Concepts of Aging—A Programmed Manual*. Washington, D.C., U.S. Government Printing Office, 1972.

### Resources

Briller BB. *Television Looks at Aging*. New York, Television Information Office, 1985.

An annotated bibliographical collection of various television shows and specials, as well as news segments highlighting issues related to health, death with dignity, coping, economics, housing, life-styles, and adapting to aging. Many of the shows are available through various news services and distribution firms. The Television Information Office, 745 Fifth Ave., New York, NY, 10151, provides reference and information services, conducts research, and serves as a link between the television industry and the public.

Brody EM, Lebowitz B: *Mental and Physical Health Practices of Older People: A Guide for Health Professionals*. New York, Springer Publishing Co., 1984.

The authors conducted inquiries outside of the doctor's office, compiling first-person accounts on the home ground of the elderly patient.

Dunkle RE, Haug M, Rosenberg M: *Communications Technology and the Elderly: Issues and Forecasts*. New York, Springer Publishing Co., 1983.

Newest developments in devices for improving the elderly's sight and hearing for increasing their access to health-care delivery, marketing, and recreational systems

Miller M: *Suicide After Sixty: The Final Alternative*. New York, Springer Publishing Co., 1979.

Pelham AO, Clark WF: *Managing Home Care for the Elderly: Lessons from Community-Based Agencies*. New York, Springer Publishing Co., 1985.

Numerous studies documenting recent experiments in providing care at home for the elderly. The research and demonstration projects that are described were funded by the Federal Health Care Financing Administration, and have had as their aim the search for alternatives to nursing home care that are appropriate and less expensive.

Phillips HT, Gaylord SA, Ibrahim M: *Aging and Public Health*. New York, Springer Publishing Co., 1985.

*Portrait of Grandpa Doc* (16 mm film). A positive message about old age. Available from Phoenix Films and Video, Inc., 468 Park Ave. South, New York, NY, 10016.

Sauer WJ, Coward RT: *Social Support Networks and the Care of the Elderly: Theory, Research, and Practice*. New York, Springer Publishing Co., 1985.

Focuses on the role of social support networks in maintaining the social, psychological, and physical well-being of the elderly.

Schulz JH: *The Economics of Aging*, 3rd ed. New York, Van Nostrand Reinhold. 1985.

Silverman PR: *Widow to Widow*. New York, Springer Publishing Co., 1985.

The story of women as widows, and widows helping widows. It summarizes recent research on the problems of widowhood. Details from the original Widow-to-Widow project are presented.

# 4

# DISEASES OF THE ELDERLY

The visible changes attributed to old age are easily recognized by society. Most people have a mental image of the stereotypical old person—wrinkled, gray-haired, stoop-shouldered, poorly dressed, and in poor health. This is inaccurate and does not truly reflect the older American in today's society. Many older persons play tennis, work full time, dress fashionably, and lead active, independent, healthy lives.

Many gerontologists believe that disease causes aging rather than vice versa. Treatment of underlying pathologic conditions will frequently remove characteristics attributed to old age. For example, the stiffened gait of an elderly arthritis victim can often be greatly improved with proper medical care. And environment, stress levels, and psychological support systems are sometimes as important as medication and diet in promoting optimal health. Nevertheless, there are physiological changes that can affect people in their later years.

Age-related physical changes occur gradually and are not always visible. They actually begin at conception and are progressive throughout life, with the continuous process of cellular growth, decay, and replacement.

It is incorrect to generalize about the physical changes of aging. Each person has individual needs and self-care requisites. For example, the situation of a poor, rural elderly person cannot be compared to that of a wealthy, urban elderly person. Each has different medical and social needs. Consider the following cases:

*Rural Poor:* An 81-year-old, undernourished, white woman, with poor dentition, productive cough, and shortness of breath. Chest X-ray and laboratory test confirm tuberculosis. She lives on a farm with her children and five grandchildren. The family is supported entirely by the farm. A recent drought has caused crop failure and poverty. The grandmother shares a bedroom with three grandchildren. There is no money for food, clothing, or medical care.

*Urban Upper-Class:* An 80-year-old, well-nourished, white woman in excellent physical and mental health with negative X-ray and laboratory findings. She lives in a condominium retirement center in Atlanta, five minutes away from her married daughter. The condominium provides inhouse nursing service, medical and dental facilities, and daily exercise classes.

These sample cases demonstrate the need for individualized care of the elderly. Whether physical problems occur singly or in combination, the important point to remember is this: Proper treatment can enable the elderly to return to optimal physical and mental health.

The rest of this chapter will cover some of the more common diseases affecting the elderly population and how those diseases can affect behavior.

## CARDIOVASCULAR DISEASE

Diseases associated with deficits of the cardiovascular system are the most common medical problems of the elderly. The aging heart experiences a decrease in cardiac output. The heart rate remains the same or slightly lower at rest in the elderly, but the heart requires more time for recovery after exertion or a stressful episode. With advancing age, the heart becomes a poorer pump, the myocardium is more irritable, and the conductive system functions less than perfectly. Blood pressure frequently rises, and the blood vessels may be sclerosed and narrowed. The renal system also suffers from this impaired circulation.

Heart disease is the leading cause of death in the United

States today. Contributing factors probably include longer life-spans, smoking, poor diet, and more sedentary lives. Cardio-vascular disease in the elderly may manifest as angina, heart attack, arrhythmias, congestive heart failure, hypertension, stroke, or peripheral vascular disease.

The elderly patient with any of these disorders may exhibit one or more of the following during acute or rehabilitative phases: social isolation, insomnia, anorexia, depressed and noncompliant behavior, despondency, or even suicide. The in-ability to work may exacerbate feelings of low self-esteem and depression, as well as contribute to economic hardship. Anxi-ety over loss of self-image and fear of death are often present.

The most important factor in dealing with the elderly car-diovascular patient is providing adequate rehabilitative pro-grams. Such programs are essential for helping the elderly pa-tient cope with changes in his or her ability to carry out the rou-tine activities of daily living.

## PULMONARY DISEASES

Significant pulmonary deficits are frequently seen in elderly pa-tients. The capacity for adequate breathing may be diminished; the efficiency of the entire respiratory system may be de-creased. Without adequate amounts of oxygen, many bodily functions are compromised. These deficits are caused by certain diseases and aggravated by smoking and prolonged exposure to polluted air in urban or occupational environments.

Pulmonary diseases common to older persons include chronic obstructive pulmonary disease (COPD), and pulmo-nary fibrosis. Single entities or a combination of diseases may be present. COPD may result from a number of different condi-tions and is ranked second only to heart disease as a cause of death or disability in the United States. It is increasing at alarm-ing rates due in part to longer life spans, better detection, in-creased smoking (especially among women), and improved survival of patients with the acute conditions that cause it.

Behavioral characteristics associated with pulmonary dis-eases may include dependence due to inability to perform activ-ities of daily living, depression, excitability, and anxiousness. When oxygen intake is decreased, confusion, weakness, and

31

irritability can result.

## MALNUTRITION

A substantial percentage of elderly persons in the United States suffer from malnutrition. Many have no one to assist them in preparing meals. Lack of desire to eat, poor income, loneliness, and poor dentition are all contributing factors to malnutrition. (See Chapter 7 for a more detailed discussion of nutrition in the elderly.)

Poor nutrition may affect all major systems and functions of the body, especially when there is a deficiency of vitamins and minerals. The cardiovascular and musculoskeletal systems can especially be affected. Behavioral manifestations may include listlessness, weakness, irritability, and depression. Elderly people living alone should be encouraged to eat with family or friends, or in other available communal situations.

## CANCER

Cancer affects all age groups, but is more common in older persons. Most cancer deaths occur over the age of 55. This may be because older persons have been exposed to carcinogens for longer periods of time. Cancer is more common in urban than rural dwellers and in males than females. Early detection remarkably improves survival rates in certain cancers.

The basic cancer treatment modalities are the same for patients of every age: surgical intervention, chemotherapy, and radiation. The type of cancer, the patient's current physical status, and other details determine the choice of therapy.

A cancer diagnosis is devastating. To most people, cancer still connotes terminal disease, mutilation, and death. Cancer patients may have to cope with changes in body image, weakness, anorexia, or sensory deprivation in intensive-care units. Stress and lowered self-esteem are often apparent. Listlessness, loneliness, and feelings of isolation frequently follow a cancer diagnosis. Anticipatory grieving can occur, especially if metastasis has been diagnosed. Shock, fear, denial, anger, and acceptance may appear in stages.

The care-giver must pay particular attention to how the patient is coping, and try to understand and encourage his or her coping mechanisms, and, in addition, provide support for the patient and family.

## PSYCHOLOGICAL DISORDERS

Most psychopathology in later life is precipitated by the crises of aging—biological, psychological, or social. These disorders are usually accompanied by feelings of loss, inferiority, and depression. (See Chapter 2 for a more complete discussion of psychopathology and aging.) A major difficulty is that many persons accept these disorders as an inevitable part of the aging process, and do not seek help until acute or severe problems appear.

Symptoms of psychological disorders in general might include withdrawal from activity, lack of interest in physical appearance, insomnia, anorexia, constipation or diarrhea, suspiciousness, hostility, delusions, feelings of inferiority, and a wide variety of somatic complaints.

## BONE AND JOINT DISEASES

Aging is frequently accompanied by increased fragility and degeneration of the bones and joints throughout the body resulting in chronic pain and diminished activity. Osteoporosis affects one out of every three women and one out of every five men over the age of 50.

In osteoporosis, the bones become weaker and thinner due to interference in the bone rebuilding process, with backache and other skeletal pain the common symptoms. Patients can be very irritable due to constant, nagging pain, may tire easily, feel weak and shaky when standing, and become extremely apprehensive about falling. Depression may result from their inability to perform daily activities because of the pain and the ensuing immobility. Osteoporosis is treated with a diet high in calcium, phosphorus, protein, vitamin D, and exercise.

Osteoarthritis can occur in any joint, but is most common in the knees, hips, and spine. Arthritis results from degeneration of cartilage that lines the joints. Treatment includes a diet high in protein and vitamins A, B, C, and E; exercise to keep the joints mobile; and medication prescribed according to the severity and the degenerative process involved. Orthopedic surgery with implantation of prosthetic joints is a last resort.

Arthritic patients may also show signs of depression resulting from pain and the inability to carry out daily activities. Immobility may cause loss of interest in themselves and the inability to cope with life patterns. Sadness and self-pity can become
paramount in the self-concept.

Arthritis is common in the elderly, and can be devastating.
It may totally change a person's ability to function in society,
especially a person who does not have a support system.

## DIABETES

Diabetes mellitus is one of the most common endocrine diseases in the United States, affecting several million people. It is
more common in those who have relatives with the disease,
and in overweight persons over the age of 40. Longer life spans,
greater public awareness, and excellent patient education programs via the family practitioner have contributed to the increase in reported cases of diabetes.

Diabetic complications may significantly affect the lives of
elderly patients. Diabetes is a leading cause of blindness in the
United States today. Chronic kidney disorders, increased sus-
ceptability to infections, peripheral neuropathy, and vascular
degeneration resulting in gangrene and loss of limbs are other
common complications.

Behavioral changes revolve around the patient's loss of
control of his or her environment. The frightening experience of
losing a limb, self-administering insulin, or the panic of being in
a world of darkness can cause fear, frustration, depression,
anxiety, and loss of self-concept. Education and counseling are
critical in helping the patient regain control of his or her life
situation—a paramount issue for the elderly.

Every person past the age of 50 should have a complete
physical examination at least annually. The checkup should be
multiphasic and include an electrocardiogram, chest X-ray,
blood studies, urinalysis, and screening for blood pressure, tuberculosis, glaucoma, oral and breast cancers, blood sugar, and
hearing deficiencies.

With proper nutrition and exercise, and with careful evaluation and treatment when necessary, the elderly can be helped

to maintain optimal health and independence.

## ALZHEIMER'S DISEASE

Dementia is *not* the name of a disease or diseases, but rather describes a wide range of symptoms of memory loss, loss of thinking, or reasoning capacity in adults. A person with a dementing illness has difficulty remembering. In the early stages, he or she may be able to conceal the symptoms very cleverly.

Alzheimer's is a type of dementia that results in impaired memory, confusion, disorientation, and eventually bizarre or inappropriate behavior. Alzheimer's is just one kind of dementia. (Chapter 7 describes other kinds of dementia.) Between three and four million persons in the United States have some degree of intellectual impairment. Alzheimer's is just one kind of dementia. In recent years, Alzheimer's disease has been much more widely publicized through the media and within the health-care professions.

Alzheimer's is a disease affecting the brain's cells. Between 25 and 30 percent of all persons who reach their mid-80s have the disease. The most common symptom is memory loss, which is accompanied by mood swings, behavior and personality changes, impaired judgment and speech, confusion, and restlessness. As the disease progresses, the victim and the victim's family become entangled in a day-to-day struggle for survival!

The earlier the onset of Alzheimer's the shorter the patient's life expectancy. For example, a patient diagnosed at age 45 may survive for ten years, while a patient diagnosed at age 65 may have a life expectancy of 20 or more years. In the final stages of the disease, death usually results from a combination of factors which are attributed to physical impairments caused by the patient's inability to eat, sleep, or even walk. The patient eventually becomes totally dependent on complete bed rest and custodial care.

In the early stages, astute family members and close friends first notice memory-loss patterns. Once a physician intervenes, appropriate tests including a CT scan will usually be required. The CT scan can help rule out other problems with similar symptoms. Additionally, an encephalography, blood studies, cerebrospinal fluid examination, and psychological and neurological tests can all help in evaluating the patient's condition.

There is no known cure for the disease. Treatment of the symptoms is the only course of action. As the disease progresses, the situation can be frightening and depressing for the patient and the family. For a patient admitted to a nursing home, the initial reaction can be extreme hostility and depression. Constant reassurance and a plan of routine care as described in Chapter 14 will help orient the patient. Because family members will undoubtedly be devastated, emotional support and counseling should be a part of the nursing home's commitment.

The Alzheimer's patient must be encouraged to eat and drink, to ensure proper nourishment. Daily exercise is equally important. Information for use by health-care agencies and personnel is available from

Alzheimer's Disease and Related Disorders
Association, Inc.
360 North Michigan Avenue.
Chicago, Illinois 60601.

Support groups for the families of Alzheimer's victims are being organized throughout the country. The Alzheimer's Disease Association national headquarters can provide lists of groups on request.

---

**Resources**

Alzheimer Abstract Service, Alzheimer's Disease and Related Disorders Association, Chicago.

A collection of easy-to-read abstracts of important research in Alzheimer's disease and related disorders. (See text for address.)

Beyers M, Durburg S, Werner J (eds): *Complete Guide to Cancer Nursing.* Oradell, NJ, Medical Economics Books, 1984.

Written, compiled, and edited by oncologic nursing specialists, but directed to the nonspecialist practicing nurse who works with cancer patients. A general overview of cancer nursing with detailed care plans for particular cancers. Essential information important for the elderly patient.

Blumenthal HT (ed): *Handbook of Diseases of Aging.* New York, Van Nostrand Reinhold, 1985.

Brink TL: *Geriatric Psychotherapy*. New York, Human Sciences Press, 1979.

Butler RN, Bearn AG (eds): *The Aging Process: Therapeutic Implications*. New York, Raven Press, 1984.

Butler RN: Paper presented at National Institute on Aging, Washington, D.C., Speakers Forum, 1976.

Cole W, Harris D: *The Elderly in America*. Boston, Allyn and Bacon, 1977.

Ebersole P, Hess P: *Toward Healthy Aging*. St. Louis, CV Mosby, 1981.

Finch CE (ed): *Handbook of the Biology of Aging*. New York, Van Nostrand Reinhold, 1985.

Gambert SR (ed): *Contemporary Geriatric Medicine*, vol 1. New York, Plenum, 1983.

Gambert SR (ed): *Contemporary Geriatric Medicine*, vol 2. New York, Plenum, 1986.

Gleckman RA, Gantz NM (eds): *Infections in the Elderly*. Boston, Little, Brown, 1983.

Hartford JT, Samorajski T (eds): *Alcoholism in the Elderly: Social and Biomedical Issues*. New York, Raven Press, 1984.

Haug MR, Ford AB, Sheafor M: *The Physical and Mental Health of Aged Women*. New York, Springer Publishing Co, 1985.
    A comprehensive assessment of the special health and social needs of older women with a marked appreciation of the great diversity of individuals within this group.

Heston LL, White JA: *Dementia: A Practical Guide to Alzheimer's Disease and Related Illnesses*. New York, WH Freeman, 1983.
    Deals with a clear examination of diseases that affect the brain, with a major discussion of Alzheimer's disease.

Mace NL, Rabins PV: *The 36-Hour Day: A Family Guide to Caring for Persons With Alzheimer's Disease, Related Dementing Illnesses, and Memory Loss in Later Life*. Baltimore, The Johns Hopkins University Press, 1981.
    A practitioner's guidebook for those professionals and family members who must who must help and serve persons suffering from dementia and related illnesses.

McCue JD: *Medical Care of the Elderly: A Practical Approach*. Lexington, MA, Collamore Press/DC Heath, 1983.

McDowell FH (ed): *Managing the Person With Intellectual Loss at Home*. White Plains, NY, Burke Rehabilitation Center, 1980.
    A 12-page handbook for families caring for persons at home who suffer from dementia or Alzheimer's disease. Available from the Burke Rehabilitation Center, White Plains, NY, 10605.

Mishara BL, Kastenbaum R: *Alcohol and Old Age*. New York, Grune & Stratton, 1980.

Moskowitz RW, Haug MR: *Arthritis and the Elderly*. New York, Springer Publishing Co, 1985.

An interdisciplinary examination of the special problems of the elderly patient with arthritis. Completely accessible to the range of professionals concerned with the care of arthritic patients.

Whitbourne SK: *The Aging Body: Physiological Changes and Psychological Consequences*. New York, Springer-Verlag, 1985.

Provides an appreciation of the complex biopsychological interactions that occur throughout adulthood and old age.

# 5

# CONFUSION

*Confusion* is characterized by a patient's disorientation to time, place, or person. Often this means that the patient cannot answer questions about who or where he or she is. A care-giver who detects a change in a patient's orientation must attempt to determine the cause. Contributing factors that can produce symptoms of confusion include electrolyte imbalance, poor diet, cardiac failure, anemia, cancer, stroke, medication side effects, hyperglycemia, hypoglycemia, hypercalcemia, hypocalcemia, and hypotension.

When confusion is being assessed, it is important to complete a careful patient history. When did the confusion first occur? How long did it last? Has the patient been on medication? The patient's physical status must be evaluated as to vital signs, skin color, and evidence of trauma. Depression can cause a significant change in a patient's orientation. A patient may become withdrawn, apathetic, listless, and lack the ability to concentrate. After careful data collection a series of laboratory tests, including a complete blood count, urinalysis, blood sugar, electrolytes, liver and serum VDRL, chest and skull X-ray, electrocardiogram, and electroencephalogram, can assist in the diagnosis.

The care-giver must react quickly to a confused patient. If detected immediately, a disoriented patient can be "turned around" by an alert staff member. If the confusion remains un-detected or untreated, the patient can progressively deteriorate to the point where the disorientation is irreversible.

## ALTERATIONS IN PERSONALITY

People who experience memory loss and confusion eventually suffer from other emotional and psychological problems. Depression is common since the confused person can be aware of the disorientation. The patient may feel sad and alone, and may have lost the ability or will to communicate with family and friends. Help must always be offered to the depressed patient. Sometimes this means simply holding the patient's hand, or accompanying him or her on a stroll through the garden or on a visit to the chapel.

Unfortunately, all too often the thought of a nursing home conjures up an image of rows of elderly men and women sitting like zombies in geriatric chairs in dark hallways. It frightens us! The stereotypical nursing home environment is often associated with confused or senile patients sitting listlessly side-by-side, never seeing the person in the next chair. Overcoming this stereotype is a real challenge requiring quality care and caring. Every effort should be made to help patients who are withdrawn, regardless of the cause. Whenever possible, the patient should be involved in the decision-making process. The patient-care plan must include achievable tasks that can be monitored and modified.

A confused patient may ramble on, repeating the same word or murmuring the same phrase hour after hour-..."flowers, flowers, flowers, flowers..."In this case, it is important to interrupt the patient and say "Mary, did you smell the flowers in the garden today?" Don't allow the patient to ramble. That only reinforces the confusion or compounds the condition.

Outbursts of anger or rage are sometimes exhibited by confused patients. The patient's anger is more a result of frustration than a serious conflict with a care-giver or event. The care-giver must learn to deal with the patient's anger by realizing that he or she is experiencing frustration, or overreacting to environmental stimuli.

Restlessness is another common emotion of the confused patient. Constant pacing, fidgeting, or swaying may be the result of an overly stimulating environment. Something as basic as too much caffeine during the day may be the cause. Sleep habits need to be evaluated, and a medication re-evaluation may be warranted.

## DEALING WITH THE FAMILY

Most families do love and care for their elderly, and want what is best for them. Accepting that a mother or father is unable to be self-sufficient and requires institutionalization because of *agnosia* (an inability to recognize persons, places, or objects), is difficult for most family members. Families generally try to provide assistance as long as possible so that an elderly family member can remain within the community, but when a dementing illness progresses, the family is faced with a tough decision. Frustration and guilt often cloud the family's ability to cope with this monumental task. Constant reassurance is necessary for both the patient and family. It is very difficult to explain and even more difficult to accept.

## THE MENTALLY RETARDED AND HANDICAPPED*

*Handicapped* is a generic term applied to persons who possess mental, physical, or sensory impairments that were diagnosed before or during the school years, and that impact on their functional abilities. The United States Department of Education estimates that over 11 percent of persons between the ages of three and 21 possess handicapping conditions such as mental retardation, speech impairments, learning disabilities, emotional disturbances, visual and hearing handicaps, and various health-related problems. Although much has been written about the education and rehabilitation of school age and the adult retarded and handicapped population, little attention has been directed toward the status of the elderly handicapped and especially the institutionalized elderly handicapped. Despite

---

*Contributed by Dennis J. Dietrich, PhD, associate professor, Department of Special Education, Kutztown University, Kutztown, PA.

professional agreement that the number of elderly handicapped is increasing, and legislative mandates now require the provision of special services, the question of how to identify the handicapped and provide quality services remains unanswered.

The elderly handicapped are susceptible to the same conditions associated with aging as their nonhandicapped peers. Their needs are similar, although individual circumstances are complicated by existing handicaps that further limit comprehension, expression, or mobility.

Care-givers in all types of institutions serving the elderly handicapped should be knowledgeable of and sensitive to the nature of the handicapped patient's condition. This can be achieved through staff training programs that address the physiological and psychological characteristics of the handicapped. These programs teach specialized techniques and procedures used in the training and care of the handicapped, and specify government agencies and advocacy groups concerned with their welfare.

Organizations involved in serving the needs of the handicapped include:

American Foundation for the Blind
15 West 16th Street
New York, NY 10011

American Speech-Language-Hearing Association
10801 Rockville Pike
Rockville, MD 20852

Association for Retarded Citizens
National Headquarters
2501 Avenue J
Arlington, TX 76011

Association for the Severely Handicapped
7010 Roosevelt Way NE
Seattle, WA 98115

National Association of the Deaf
814 Thayer Avenue
Silver Spring, MD 20910

United Cerebral Palsy Associations, Inc.
66 East 34th Street
New York, NY 10016

---

**Resources**

Beasley DS, Davis GA (eds): *Aging: Communication Processes and Disorders*. New York, Grune & Stratton, Inc, 1981.

*Confusion and the Elderly* (16 mm film). A 40 minute color film featuring an acutely confused elderly lady. Reactions of neighbors and friends are interpreted from the patient's viewpoint. Available from Duke-Watts Family Medicine Program, 407 Crutchfield Street, Durham, NC, 27704.

DiGiovanni L: The elderly handicapped: A little known group. *Gerontologist* 1978;18:262-266.

Edelson J, Lyons W: *Institutional Care of the Mentally Impaired Edlerly*. New York, Van Nostrand Reinhold, 1984.
    An excellent resource that provides ideas to the professional staff for helping an often neglected group of patients.

Fisk AA: *A New Look at Senility: It's Causes, Diagnosis, Treatment, and Management*. Springfield, IL, Charles C. Thomas Publisher, 1981.

Goldstein G, Ruthven L: *Rehabilitation of the Brain-Damaged Adult*. New York, Plenum, 1983.

Segal R: Trends in services for the aged mentally retarded. *Mental Retardation* 1977;15:25-27.

Wolanin MO, Phillips LRF: *Confusion: Prevention and Care*. St. Louis, CV Mosby, 1981.
    Although out of print, an excellent source on confusion available in many university libraries.

# 6

# DRUG THERAPY IN THE ELDERLY

## MULTIPLE MEDICATIONS

Elderly persons are frequently treated for more than one chronic condition simultaneously, sometimes by different physicians. It is essential that physicians and pharmacists instruct elderly patients to keep complete lists of all medications being taken at any given time, plus records of drugs taken during the previous 12 months, since the effects of some drugs with long half-lives may persist in the body long after the last dose is taken. This information will give the physician a more complete picture of the elderly patient's health status, aid in diagnosis and treatment, and help prevent harmful drug interactions.

Drugs should be used with more than usual care in the elderly. Altered renal or hepatic function, metabolic changes, and chronic illnesses may affect the action of drugs in the body. Medications should be prescribed only when the potential benefits to the patient outweigh the potential harmful effects.

## PATIENT COMPLIANCE PROBLEMS

It seems ironic that a patient will make the effort to see a doctor and have a prescription filled, but neither follow the doctor's advice nor take the medication as directed. Yet, lack of compliance is not unusual.

There are many reasons for noncompliance—confusion

over complicated multiple-drug regimens, the inability to clearly read prescription labels, forgetfulness, dissatisfaction with the treatment received, drug side effects, and cost. Some patients simply cannot swallow capsules; others insist that tablets stick in their throats. A patient may declare that the tablet form of a medication is much more effective than the capsule form of the same drug. Patients have been known to spit out medications given in any form other than liquid.

Drug-taking behavior should be integrated with the patient's daily routine. The specific times for taking medication, the relationship of doses to food, and whether to "make up" missed doses, should be discussed. Drug regimens should be simplified to doses taken once or twice daily where possible, but certain drugs must be given more frequently. Be aware that patients often take a drug half as frequently as prescribed because of fear of being over-medicated or addicted.

A pill organizer, which can be bought at the pharmacy, is a very helpful aid to the patient. It functions as a bookkeeping system so the patient can tell if he has taken his medication for the day. An organizer needn't even be purchased. An empty egg carton, with the compartments labeled with the days of the week, is just as functional. Other useful compliance aids are watches with alarms that can be set for medication administration times, or pill boxes with built-in alarms. Pill splitters are helpful for some patients who have difficulty using a knife to cut scored tablets.

If self-medicating, patients should be checked to determine if they can read the label on the bottle, tell the difference between their tablets (as many different types of tablets are white), and are capable of opening the child-proof cap. The label should clearly indicate whether the medication should be taken "as needed," or in a specific amount at a particular time. Proper storage of medication, away from heat and moisture, or refrigeration, should also be discussed. When visiting the doctor, patients should bring all their pills with them—including the ones they buy without a prescription. Drugs such as nitroglycerin, which lose potency rapidly, should be discarded after the expiration date.

It is important for pharmacists, physicians, and other

health professionals to warn patients against taking tablets or capsules too large for their swallowing ability. Other guidelines include:

- Solid dosage forms should never be taken without a liquid. Pills should never be "dry-mouthed." A minimum of three ounces of liquid should be swallowed for proper disintegration and dissolution in the gastrointestinal tract.
- Some liquid should be taken first, to wet the throat before the pill is swallowed.
- In many cases, capsules that are difficult to swallow may be opened and the contents taken as a powder. However, it is advisable not to open capsules containing timed-release pellets, because it is difficult to ensure that contents will not be crushed or chewed.
- Some tablets may be crushed or broken if needed, to make them easier to swallow. *CAUTION:* Time-released tablets should never be crushed. This may allow too much drug to reach the circulation at one time. Other tablets that should not be crushed include enteric-coated tablets and uncoated tablets designed to dissolve in the mouth.
- Patients should never take any medication while laughing or talking. Full attention should be directed to swallowing.
- Water (or another liquid) should always be taken before swallowing viscous or irritating liquids such as cough syrups or citric acid preparations. Medications of this type may produce coughing spasms that can be harmful, especially to a patient with a history of heart attack. A little water taken first may help suppress the coughing reflex.
- Many patients do not use inhalers properly. The timing of the inhalation in relation to the breathing cycle and the distance of the inhaler from the mouth are critical. Special devices are available in pharmacies for patients who have difficulty with their technique.

## EFFECTS OF MEDICATION ON THE ELDERLY

The elderly have more chronic illnesses and take more medications than do younger people. This "polypharmacy" produces a greater likelihood of adverse side effects, drug interactions, and contraindications between drugs and disease states other

47

than the one the drug is treating. For example, certain antihypertensive medications may worsen a patient's asthma. Even eyedrops and topical drugs, such as creams and ointments, may have untoward effects on a distant organ system.

Some elderly patients cannot tolerate drugs that may cause seemingly minor changes in blood pressure, electrolyte balance, or body temperature. The elderly have altered homeostatic mechanisms. For example, a diuretic may cause sodium loss which the kidneys cannot correct, and the patient may feel lethargic, nauseated, or even have a seizure.

Overuse of medication in the elderly can be contributed to an overzealous prescriber, as well as an elderly person who is trying to treat all his own aches and pains. Sometimes the number of medications being taken at one time can mount up, and do more harm than good. While the average elderly patient takes three to five medications daily, some take as many as ten to 20. In many cases such large drug regimens can be evaluated and pared down to the essentials, with those medications that are ineffective eliminated completely.

It should be recognized that all the ingredients in a drug product are not written on the label. Elderly patients may take elixirs with high alcohol content, diabetics may take medication containing high quantities of sugar, and patients with hypertension, congestive heart disease, and kidney disease may take medications containing large amount of sodium. Even the dyes in some drugs can cause severe reactions in patients who are aspirin-intolerant. Information on ingredients not listed on the label may be obtained from the pharmacy or from the drug manufacturer.

*Changes in drug absorption.* While several age-related changes occur in the gastrointestinal tract, most drugs are absorbed better in the elderly than in younger patients. However, the rate of drug absorption in the older person may be slower, and can result in a delayed onset of effect for some drugs. Oral liquid dosage forms may speed up the onset of drug action, and are useful in patients with swallowing difficulties, feeding tubes, ileostomies and high colostomies, and patients who may "cheek" their medications.

Food may modify the absorption of some drugs. Food increases propranolol and hydralazine absorption, for example, and diminishes the absorption of certain antibiotics, such as penicillin, ampicillin, some of the tetracyclines, and erythromycins. These drugs should be taken one hour before, or two hours after a meal. Taking medication after meals is a useful technique to reduce gastrointestinal discomfort caused by many drugs, as long as the absorption isn't compromised. It is a good general recommendation for the patient to take chronic medications in the same relation to meals all the time.

Certain drugs may reduce the absorption of other drugs: examples of these are antacids, psyllium (a bulk-forming laxative), colestipol, cholestyramine, and drugs with anticholinergic side effects, such as many antidepressants, major tranquilizers, and antiparkinson medications.

Absorption of intramuscular and subcutaneous injections may be delayed in the elderly, especially in those with poor circulation from diabetes or peripheral vascular disease. Intramuscular injections can be painful in patients with reduced muscle mass.

*Changes in drug distribution.* The elderly have more body fat, less muscle, and less body water than young people, and consequently drug distribution may be different. Drug binding to serum albumin is reduced in the elderly and more unbound or "active" drug may be available to the drug receptor sites.

*Changes in drug elimination.* Metabolism of some drugs is slowed down in the elderly. Examples of some drugs that require a dose reduction because of reduced metabolism are certain antidepressants, quinidine, phenytoin, and lidocaine.

Kidney elimination is reduced in the elderly, and is important for drugs excreted primarily by the kidneys: aminoglycoside antibiotics, digoxin, cimetidine, and lithium, to name a few.

In general, for many drugs, the doses used in the elderly need to be lower than in their middle-aged counterparts, largely because of reduced metabolism and kidney excretion.

## COMMON DRUG SIDE EFFECTS

The elderly seem to be predisposed to certain side effects from drugs. Sometimes these are dose-related and can be eliminated by dosage reduction. Many drug reactions affect mood, cognitive function, energy level, or behavior of the elderly.

Some drugs can actually produce dementia-like symptoms. This can be from a toxic dose of drugs, such as digoxin, cimetidine, levodopa, quinidine, nonsteroidal anti-inflamatory agents, corticosteroids, and many others. Every drug that has pharmacologic activity in the brain has the potential for causing dementia. The confusion caused by drugs is usually much more rapid in onset than that caused by Alzheimer's disease or multi-infarct dementia. Sometimes a drug may cause confusion indirectly by lowering blood sugar or modifying body salts.

Drugs may also cause depression. Certain antihypertensive medications are particularly noted for this. Drugs may clearly modify sexual function, affecting libido, erection, and ejaculation. Drugs can produce weakness by modifying body salts. Many drugs produce drowsiness, particularly central nervous system depressants such as tranquilizers. Insomnia is frequently caused by theophylline, a drug used for treating lung diseases. Alcohol, in combination with many drugs, will predispose to vasodilation, causing dizziness or fainting, low blood sugar, confusion, seizures or hyperexcitability. Hallucinations may be caused by antihypertensive agents and cardiac drugs, which are not usually thought of as having pharmacologic activity within the brain.

Tremors may be caused by certain drugs, such as those used in asthma. A movement disorder, such as mouth movements, caused by neuroleptic drugs (tardive dyskinesia) may appear to be a sign of senility or a behavioral problem to the uninformed, but is actually a drug side effect. The seizure-threshold may be lowered by drugs such as penicillins, antidepressants, and major tranquilizers.

Allergic reactions to medication do not appear to increase in the elderly. Allergic reactions are not usually dose-related and can result from even a very small dose of a drug. Symptoms may include rash, pruritis, shortness of breath, fainting, and even harmful effects to the liver or kidney. Many patients mistakenly think that they are allergic to a medication when they tolerate the side effects poorly, such as patients who become nauseated after taking codeine.

When evaluating drugs as possible culprits in an unexplained or adverse reaction, look carefully at when drugs were started and stopped, when dosage increments occurred and, if possible, find out how long it might take for the drug to fully accumulate or leave the body. Some drugs have long "half-lives" and the toxic effect from such a drug may not be apparent for a few weeks after it was started. Drugs that cause tardive dyskinesia may only show that effect after the drug dose has been lowered, or completely discontinued.

## NONPRESCRIPTION DRUGS

Most of the drugs in the typical home medicine cabinet are nonprescription or over-the-counter (OTC) drugs. Self-treatment with OTC drugs occurs frequently among the elderly because many elderly persons with limited incomes cannot afford physicians' or emergency room fees. Medicaid and Medicare can often help, but certain federal regulations can sometimes make it difficult for patients to receive all the medical help they feel they need. Elderly patients cannot always arrange for office visits at convenient times, or may have difficulty finding transportation. And many people simply take the path of least resistance. The powerful influence of advertising via television, radio, or the print media cannot be minimized. Individuals who have afflictions, real or imaginary, may often purchase a product they have seen in an advertisement.

It is estimated that expenditures for OTC drugs increase with age. Persons over age 65 in this country spend one third of their medication dollar on OTC drugs. Studies have shown that the elderly frequently use nonprescription analgesics, antacids, cough and cold preparations, laxatives, and vitamins. Most often, they do not consult physicians about their use.

## OTC ANALGESICS

Aspirin is the most frequently used nonprescription analgesic. It is estimated that over 200 OTC preparations contain it. Some trade names and advertisements for aspirin-containing products give no indication that aspirin is an ingredient. This can easily cause confusion for an elderly person who wishes to avoid aspirin and is not in the habit of reading product labels.

For example, an elderly woman in New Orleans, who had been instructed by her physician to avoid aspirin, declared, "I don't take aspirin, I take Anacin instead!" (Though Anacin-3 is aspirin-free, aspirin is the main ingredient in regular Anacin.)

Though aspirin is by no means physically addicting , psychological dependency has occurred. A 72-year-old Boston nursing-home resident, for example, took two aspirin every night at bedtime, insisting he could not get to sleep without it. Yet aspirin has no sedative properties.

As an analgesic, aspirin ranks high. Its antipyretic and anti-inflammatory properties further increase its usefulness. But there are potential problems. Hypersensitivity reactions, gastrointestinal blood loss, and drug interactions, especially with oral anticoagulants and uricosuric agents, may occur. See the table for some of the more significant drug interactions involving salicylates.

Symptoms of overdose or toxicity appear at lower doses in the elderly than in younger people. Irritability, confusion, and deafness may appear quickly. Hepatic toxicity is dose-related. Dyspepsia occurs in a small number of patients, especially in those with rheumatoid arthritis. Salicylates may cause decreased sodium and chloride excretion, which can lead to edema. This possibility is of special concern to patients on low-sodium diets or with congestive heart failure.

Chronic use of aspirin or any salicylate may cause a decrease in iron reserves due to blood loss associated with gastrointestinal irritation. Since older people are frequently suffering from iron-deficiency anemia anyway, this can complicate an existing problem. Patients with anemia should avoid aspirin if possible. One to four aspirin tablets (5 grains each) can prolong bleeding time by several minutes. Intake of nine 5-grain tablets a day can cause as much as 6 ml of blood loss daily. Fifteen percent of patients lose 10 ml, or 2 teaspoons daily. Chronic aspirin use has been associated with chronic ulceration. This in turn creates a need for another product often overused by the elderly—*antacids.*

The following case is not unusual: A Philadelphia patient complained of pain when swallowing as well as pain in the lower intestinal tract. She was given a complete physical examina-

| DRUG INTERACTIONS INVOLVING SALICYLATES | |
|---|---|
| DRUG | EFFECT WITH SALICYLATE |
| Alkalinizers, urinary | Increased excretion and decreased effect of salicylates |
| Aminosalicylic acid (PAS) | Increased possibility of salicylate toxicity |
| Anticoagulants | Enhanced anticoagulant effect |
| Corticosteroids | Increased danger of gastrointestinal ulceration |
| Methotrexate | Increased methotrexate toxicity |
| Phenobarbital | Decreased effect of salicylates due to enzyme induction |
| NSAIDS | Increased danger of gastrointestinal ulceration |
| Phenytoin | Increased phenytoin effect |
| Probenecid | Antagonism of the uricosuric effect of probenecid |
| Sulfinpyrazone | Antagonism of the uricosuric effect of sulfinpyrazone |
| Sulfonylureas | Enhanced hypoglycemic effect of the sulfonylureas |

tion by a gastroenterologist, who found an irritated esophagus and small intestine. The patient's history included long-term daily intake of an effervescent aspirin-containing product. Such long-term use was contrary to the instructions on the label. The patient was advised to stop taking aspirin products, and her condition improved.

Aspirin should be avoided in those patients taking nonsteroidal anti-inflammatory agents. Studies have shown that the anti-inflammatory response of the nonsteroidal anti-inflammatory agent is decreased when used concomitantly with aspirin products. Gastrointestinal bleeding and ulceration are enhanced when both agents are used together.

Though aspirin is still the most-used drug in America, acetaminophen is quickly becoming a popular substitute when analgesic and/or antipyretic actions are needed. But acetaminophen is not an anti-inflammatory, as aspirin is, and is not as effective for rheumatoid arthritis. Acetaminophen has some advantages: It will not produce gastric irritation or erosion, as aspirin can, and does not cause occult blood loss.

Although acetaminophen is not effective in severe pain, its effect may be enhanced by increasing the dosage to 1000 mg. Larger doses do not enhance analgesia but increase the toxicity of acetaminophen. Toxic doses can sometimes be fatal. In Great Britain, more than 5000 persons are admitted to hospitals each year due to acetaminophen over-dosage. Fifty to 100 of those patients die. Acetaminophen poisoning is also becoming common in this country. Chronic high doses of acetominophen may be toxic to patients with alcoholism and liver damage.

## ANTACIDS

Twenty percent of Americans suffer from acid indigestion or "heartburn," and the majority of those sufferers treat themselves with OTC antacids, sometimes indiscriminantly.

Many available antacid products are safe and effective when used as directed. But abuse of these products is not uncommon. For example, one 72-year-old St. Louis-area man regularly drank antacid right out of the bottle without measuring the doses. He was self-treating what be believed to be ulcers. He complained of being "very nervous" and worried a great deal about unlikely and inappropriate things—such as his town running out of water during the summer, and the water pipes freezing in the mobile trailer in which he no longer lived. In short, his problems were mostly imagined. But the stress in his life caused many physiological problems including "heartburn." This patient bought antacids by the case and relied on them daily. This kind of excessive use accounts for a total of $500 million in antacid sales in the United States each year.

Many elderly people rely on sodium bicarbonate (baking soda) as an antacid. It cannot be denied that sodium bicarbonate does an excellent job of neutralizing excess acid (as well as needed acid). But it causes acid-rebound: Acid production is greater after taking sodium bicarbonate than it was before. There is also some systemic absorption that can upset the acid-base balance, causing alkalosis. For these reasons, sodium bicarbonate should be reserved for occasional use only.

The following case illustrates how harmful the overuse of bicarbonate can be : A 76-year-old Seattle man habitually took a teaspoonful of baking soda every night at bedtime. During the night he would get up frequently to take further doses to relieve his upset stomach. The patient died at 78 from massive ulcerations of the stomach and problems associated with disturbed acid-base balance.

Anyone who takes any type of antacid should heed the warnings found on the labels of most major brands. The warnings include:

- Do not take more than [specified dose] in a 24-hour period or use for longer than two weeks except under the advice and supervision of a physician. (A patient who needs antacids for longer periods may actually have a pathological condition requiring diagnosis and treatment by a physician.)
- Do not use this product if you have kidney disease except under the advice and supervision of a physician. (OTC antacids may contain more than 25mEq potassium per daily dosage. The magnesium or aluminum may also be harmful.)
- Do not use this product if you are on a sodium-restricted diet, except under the advice and supervision of a physican. (Many products contain more than 5mEq sodium per daily dosage.)

Antacids may have laxative or constipating effects that can add to existing bowel disturbances so common among the elderly. Labels should be checked carefully. Products found to have laxative effects in greater than 5 percent of patients must carry the warning : "may have a laxative effect." Products causing constipation in greater than 5 percent must warn: "may cause constipation." A patient who has a problem with a particular product may be better off trying an alternative.

The most significant antacid drug interaction involves tetracycline. When antacid comes in contact with free tetracycline in the intestine, the absorption of tetracycline can be decreased by 50 to 100 percent, significantly interfering with the intended antibiotic therapy. Antacids should generally be avoided during tetracycline therapy; many antacid product labels carry warnings to that effect.

The taste factor is very important in patient compliance

with antacid therapy, and personal preference may be followed when possible. Other helpful guidelines for antacid therapy include the following:

- Liquid and powder forms are more effective than tablets because dispersion in the stomach is faster and surface area is greater.
- Tablets generally taste better than liquids because of the decreased surface area.
- If tablets are used, they should be thoroughly chewed or dissolved in the mouth before swallowing. Tablets swallowed whole are much less effective in neutralizing acid.

## COUGH AND COLD PREPARATIONS

There is general agreement that OTC cough and cold remedies can be effective in relieving the symptoms of the common cold. But they are not without risk.

Cold preparations containing *antihistamines* can cause drowsiness and have been implicated in car accidents.

Preparations containing *anticholinergics*, such as the belladonna alkaloids, may cause excessively dry mouth, constipation, insomnia, excitement, confusion, rapid pulse, or blurred vision. If any of these side effects appear, the medication should be discontinued. Patients with asthma, prostate enlargement, or angle-closure glaucoma should avoid anticholinergics. Patients already taking drugs with anticholinergic effects, such as phenothiazines, antiparkinsonism drugs, and tricyclic antidepressants, are much more likely to develop side effects when OTC anticholinergics are added.

Preparations containing *sympathomimetic amines*, which are used for their bronchodilating and decongestant properties, may induce dizziness, nervousness, and insomnia in elderly persons. Diabetics taking these preparations may require insulin dosage adjustments. These agents may cause drug interactions and exacerbate hypertension and certain cardiac problems. Large amounts of these drugs, such as phenylpropanolamine, are found in diet pills. They may cause confusion, high blood pressure, and seizures.

Many *cough suppressants* contain large amounts of sugar and are contraindicated in diabetes. Cough medicines should *not* be used for chronic problems, such as asthma or emphysema, in which cough relief may cause harmful retention of respiratory secretions.

The side effects mentioned above can occur at normal, recommended doses. Problems are even more likely in people who drink right from cough syrup bottles without measuring doses, or who otherwise exceed recommended limits.

## LAXATIVES

Laxatives are one of the most used and abused classes of drugs, especially among the elderly. They cannot be considered totally safe or harmless. They are habit-forming drugs and are one of the most frequent *causes* of constipation.

Stimulant laxatives produce bowel evacuation by artificial over-stimulation of the intestinal tract. This keeps the bowel muscles from doing their job. With prolonged laxative use, natural peristalsis can diminish, as bowel muscles become lazy and inactive, and begin to atrophy. Chronic constipation results. This problem has been known to have significant effects on the behavior of elderly patients.

Other types of laxatives are less likely to cause dependency, and should be given preference when possible. Bulk-forming laxatives, such as the psyllium-containing preparations, work by expanding during contact with water. The intestinal tract responds in a natural manner to the increased presure they cause. This allows for a natural bowel movement without harm to the tone of the bowels. Nevertheless, no laxative is right for every situation. Careful evaluation of the individual patient is necessary to select the best laxative.

Many people believe that a bowel movement is necessary for proper health. They must be educated regarding normal bowel frequency: It can vary from three times daily to three times weekly.

The following case illustrates how a pattern of laxative abuse can develop: A 72-year-old woman experienced an attack of diarrhea and took an OTC antidiarrheal (kaolin/pectin) product. Twenty-four hours later, she decided to take some milk of magnesia because she felt constipated and had not yet had a bowel movement that day. Such excessive concern over bowel habits can lead to irrational behavior and self-preoccupation, as well as actual physical harm.

Most experts agree that laxatives are indicated only in unusual circumstances. Valid indications may include:

- Necessity to avoid straining.
- Coronery artery disease.
- Aortic aneurysm.
- Cerebrovascular accident.
- Partial or complete loss of rectal reflex.
- Altered bowel motility caused by drug therapy.
- Atrophied abdominal and perineal muscles.
- Diminished food intake.

If none of the above is present, then laxative use should be carefully evaluated, especially if any of the following are present: fecal incontinence, mental disturbance, intestinal obstruction, urine retention, or rectal bleeding.

The goal of every elderly person should be to keep the intestinal tract in as good condition and tone as possible. This is best accomplished with a diet high in fiber and relatively low in meat, adequate daily fluid intake, and regular exercise. Intestinal tone is also aided by avoiding laxative use unless it is absolutely necessary.

Nonprescription medications can often enhance an elderly person's comfort and well-being. But they should be used with caution—not only because of possible side effects or toxicity, but also because they can sometimes mask symptoms of a serious underlying disorder requiring more aggressive treatment by a physician. Because of the special problems of the elderly, that advice is probably more important for them than for any other age group.

**Resources**

Abel L: *Psychoactive Drugs and Sex.* Plenum Publishing Corp., New York, 1985.

Bassuk EL, Schoonover SC, Gelenberg AJ (eds): *The Practitioner's Guide to Psychoactive Drugs.* Plenum Publishing Corp., New York, 1983.

MacLennam WJ, Shepard AN, Stevenson IH: *The Elderly.* Springer-Verlag, Inc., New York, 1984.
    Special attention is given to practical problems involved in giving drugs to the elderly. The pharmacokinetics and pharmacodynamics of drugs in

old age is discussed. Provides a clear understanding of drug treatment of the elderly patient relative to clinical pharmacology and geriatric medicine.

Melzack R: *Pain Measurement and Assessment.* Raven Press, New York, 1983.

Sloan RW: *Practical Geriatric Therapeutics.* Medical Economics Books, Oradell, NJ, 1986.
   Provides a rational framework for selecting drugs and tailoring drug therapy to the specific needs of the elderly patient. Emphasizes th use of drugs in an ambulatory or nursing home setting.

United States Department of Health, Education, and Welfare: *Long term care facility improvement campaign.* DHEW Publ. No. (OS) 76-50050. U.S. Government Printing Office, Washington, D.C., 1976.

Walker, O: Unpublished observations, 1969-1986.

# 7

## NUTRITION IN THE ELDERLY

Nutrition has a major role in the proper health care of the elderly. Too many older people rely exclusively on synthetic or natural medicines to cure their aches and pains, while overlooking the importance of proper diet, vitamin supplements, and adequate physical exercise.

Malnutrition is a frequent contributor to morbidity and mortality in the elderly. It decreases immunocompetence, rendering patients much more susceptible to infection and disease. Malnourished institutionalized patients are highly susceptible to non-healing bedsores and decubitus ulcers.

### FACTORS CONTRIBUTING TO MALNUTRITION

The prevalence of malnutrition in the elderly can be attributed to a number of factors, including:

*Chronic drug use.* Diuretics may increase the need for potassium, magnesium, and zinc. Aspirin in large doses, as may be prescribed for rheumatoid arthritis, increases the need for vitamin C. Since many medications may also dull the appetite, the drug regimen should be carefully reviewed in cases of suspected malnutrition.

*Illness.* Chronic ailments such as heart conditions, digestive tract problems, poor teeth or gums, and a wide range of dietary restrictions can cause severe nutritional problems. In addition, emotional problems may cause diminished appetite, resulting in poor nutrition.

*Ignorance of proper diet.* Many older people are unaware of what constitutes a proper diet. Ongoing educational programs are needed—both in institutions and for the general public. Americans have become "fast-food" junkies, and many people, including the elderly, are guilty of forsaking well-balanced meals for food that is fast and convenient. Excessive intake of alcoholic beverages or soft drinks can also interfere with proper nutrition by diminishing the desire for food and altering hunger patterns.

*Financial and logistical problems.* Because of fixed, limited incomes, many elderly people can't afford proper, well-balanced diets. In isolated rural communities, many don't have adequate transportation to and from grocery stores. Urban dwellers living alone are often afraid to venture out of their immediate neighborhoods to get to large supermarkets, relying instead on nearby convenience markets and frozen or precooked meals.

*Reduced sense of taste and smell.* Very old persons are often less conscious of hunger because of reduced sensitivity to flavor and odor. This can lead to reduced stomach activity. Between the ages of 30 and 75, the reduction in taste buds or capacity for tasting may be as much as 60 percent.

*Secondary malnutrition.* Poor digestive processes are not uncommon in the elderly. Certain disorders of the esophagus, including spasms, cancer, hiatal hernia, or diverticulitis, may retard the passage of food to the stomach. Hypermotility of the stomach and hypomotility of the intestinal tract are common. Hypoactive salivary glands may diminish the digestive process. Digestive enzyme activity may be lacking in the stomach, pancreas, and small intestine. The liver and biliary system may be producing less bile. All these factors lead to stomach problems and abdominal pain.

Atherosclerosis and circulatory diseases may interfere with the proper distribution of nutrients to body cells. Because of loss of storage cells, foods may provide only short-term benefit. Metabolism, especially of minerals and electrolytes, may be altered due to tissue changes. With aging, increased loss of muscle and kidney function can contribute to increased protein loss.

## OBESITY

Over 50 percent of the American population is overweight to some extent. Our tendency to lead sedentary lives contributes to this dubious distinction.

The following is a somewhat extreme example of an all-too-common syndrome: A 70-year-old woman living in Los Angeles cooked continuously, using saturated fat as seasoning. Her specialties were cakes and pies with plenty of sugar. She usually ate as much as she served her friends and relatives, until she tipped the scales at 290 pounds. Her obesity, coupled with her sedentary life, eventually caused her "early" death. Her death was directly attributed to her lifestyle and bad habits, which resulted in a state of ultimate deterioration.

Obesity is actually a type of malnutrition. Six of the ten leading causes of death in the United States—heart disease, cancer, stroke, diabetes, arteriosclerosis, and cirrhosis of the liver—are linked directly to dietary habits, primarily the overconsumption of *saturated fats, cholesterol, sugar, salt,* and *alcohol.*

Since 1909, fat consumption has increased over 25 percent. Fat now accounts for almost 42 percent of caloric intake in the average American diet. Caloric intake from carbohydrates has decreased 9 percent, but much of it comes from sugar and alcohol. Alcohol, fats, and sugar are low in vitamins and minerals, and malnutrition can result from an overconsumption of them.

## DIETARY RECOMMENDATIONS

Cholesterol consumption should not exceed 300 mg per day. Since a medium-size egg contains approximately 300 mg of cholesterol, this recommendation presents a real challenge to many people.

It is estimated that Americans consume 85 percent more salt than is needed in their daily diets. Recommended total daily intake is 3 g, approximately the amount in two hot dogs. New habits must be learned—for example, it is not necessary to add salt to food before, during, or after cooking.

Other hints for healthful dining include:

- Fruits and vegetables, especially those with high fiber content, should be an important part of the daily diet.

- More poultry and fish should be added to the diet, and consumption of other types of meat curtailed.
- Nonfat milk should be substituted for whole milk. But note that low-fat milk contains much higher concentrations of sodium than does whole milk.
- Alcoholic beverages should be limited.
- Refined sugar should be limited or avoided.
- Cholesterol should be reduced; eggs should be limited.
- Baked or broiled foods should be favored over foods that are fried.
- Salt should be limited.
- Foods containing additives (preservatives, coloring agents, etc.) should be avoided or drastically limited.

Caloric intake should be spaced evenly throughout the day. A person who eats no breakfast and very little lunch can still gain weight. An excessive intake of carbohydrates at the evening meal can't be converted to energy at one time and will, instead, be converted in the liver to fat, causing weight gain. This is why the after-dinner stroll is a good practice, especially when the meal is high in carbohydrates.

## AGE – RELATED CHANGES

Although the nutritional needs of the elderly may not be age-related, it can be shown that:

- A 75-year-old man has a metabolic rate approximately 15 percent lower than that of a 30-year-old man.
- Total body water decreases by about 18 percent from age 30 to age 75.
- The proportion of body fat to body weight may increase with age. Increase of body fat with a proportionate decrease in body lean is undesirable.
- In men, energy expenditure decreases 21 percent between age 20 and age 74, and 31 percent between age 75 and age 99.
- Caloric requirements are lessened in the elderly because of lower basal metabolism and decreased physical activity.
- For many reasons, appetite is often diminished in very old persons, leading to reduced intake of nutrients.

Throughout the United States today, there is a growing awareness of good health practices, especially among the young. Our fascination with jogging, walking, aerobics, health clubs, organic gardening, and so on, have positive health effects. Unfortunately, these trends have not had a great effect on the elderly, especially those who are institutionalized.

## NUTRITIONAL NEEDS

The Food and Nutrition Board of the National Academy of Sciences has provided Recommended Daily Dietary Allowances (RDA) for certain vitamins and minerals based on current research data. The recommendations for men and women over age 50 are reproduced in the accompanying table.

A discussion of some specific nutrients follows:

*Calcium.* Calcium is needed to maintain normal bone density. Adults who have symptoms of osteoporosis should receive at least 1000 mg daily. One cup of whole milk contains 285 mg of calcium; one cup of skim milk has 300 mg. Calcium loss may be the cause of many lower back pain complaints which is greater in patients confined to beds or wheelchairs.

*Iron.* Iron is required for the synthesis of hemoglobin and myoglobin and is needed in the diet at all ages. The best food sources of iron are fish and meat (fish is preferred). The iron in eggs, spinach, and some other vegetables forms insoluble salts with phosphates and phytates, making much of it unavailable for absorption.

Advertising claims have convinced many elderly persons that over-the-counter iron preparations will give them real pep. But in a normal person with adequate iron stores, only 10 percent of the iron in iron-containing preparations or foods will actually be absorbed.

Caution must be observed in using iron supplements. There is a limit to the amount of iron the body can store, and excessive amounts can lead to iron storage disease and liver damage. This is not uncommon in the elderly who take iron supplements without proper guidance and care.

*Zinc.* Zinc is necessary for growth and is vital component of many essential body enzymes. It seems to accelerate wound healing and may be beneficial for treating pressure sores in bedridden patients. Dietary fiber increases the need for zinc by decreasing its availability.

## RECOMMENDED DAILY DIETARY ALLOWANCES

|  | Males Over Age 50 | Females Over Age 50 |
|---|---|---|
| FAT-SOLUBLE VITAMINS |  |  |
| Vitamin A (retinol equivalents)[1] | 1,000 R E | 800 R E |
| Vitamin D (micrograms of cholecalciferol)[2] | 5 $\mu$g | 5 $\mu$g |
| Vitamin E (milligrams of alpha-tocopherol equivalents)[3] | 10 mg | 8 mg |
| WATER-SOLUBLE VITAMINS |  |  |
| Vitamin C | 60 mg | 60 mg |
| Thiamin (vitamin $B_1$) | 1.2 mg | 1.0 mg |
| Riboflavin (vitamin $B_2$) | 1.4 mg | 1.2 mg |
| Niacin (milligrams of niacin equivalents)[4] | 16 mg | 13 mg |
| Folacin | 0.4 mg | 0.4 mg |
| Vitamin $B_6$ | 2.2 mg | 2.0 mg |
| Vitamin $B_{12}$ | 3.0 $\mu$g | 3.0 $\mu$g |
| MINERALS |  |  |
| Calcium | 800 mg | 800 mg |
| Phosphorus | 800 mg | 800 mg |
| Iodine | 150 $\mu$g | 150 $\mu$g |
| Iron | 10 mg | 10 mg |
| Magnesium | 350 mg | 300 mg |
| Zinc | 15 mg | 15 mg |

[1] 1 retinol equivalent = 1 $\mu$g retinol or 6 $\mu$g $\beta$-carotene.
[2] 5 $\mu$g cholecalciferol = 200 I U vitamin D.
[3] 1 mg $d$-$\alpha$-tocopherol = 1 $\alpha$-tocopherol equivalent.
[4] 1 niacin equivalent = 1 mg of niacin or 60 mg of dietary tryptophan.
Adapted from *Recommended Dietary Allowances*, Ninth Edition (1980), with the permission of the National Academy of Sciences, Washington, D.C.

*Potassium.* Potassium deficiency is not unusual among older persons. An elderly man or woman needs about 60 mEq per day, and an insufficient intake may cause muscle weakness, apathy or depression, cramps, fecal impaction, constipation, paralytic ileus, and decreased cardiac output. In severe, prolonged potassium depletion, the cells in the kidneys, heart, and skeletal muscles may be irreversibly damaged.

Sufficient amounts of potassium can be obtained solely from dietary sources. Potassium-rich foods include oranges, bananas, apricots, and many other fruits and vegetables.

Potassium supplements are rarely required and should be used with caution. Large doses can cause potassium intoxication, with symptoms such as sharp or persistant abdominal discomfort, stiffening of the fingers, and metallic taste. If symptoms occur, potassium supplementation should be discontinued immediately.

*Protein.* Healthy elderly men need at least 56 g of protein daily; healthy elderly women, 46 g. Protein requirements are greater in the elderly, because hypochlorhydia frequently diminishes their ability to absorb nutrients. Since the elderly often have limited nutritional reserves, the effects of stress caused by fever, malabsorption, indigestion, or poor metabolism can create a greater demand for protein.

*Carbohydrates.* Carbohydrates should provide at least 58 percent of the total energy from the diet. As a rule, carbohydrate intake should decrease with increasing age; however, too great a decrease can cause any of the following problems:

- Loss of tissue protein.
- Rise in blood cholesterol due to mobilization of fat.
- Lack of energy due to electrolyte imbalance caused by increased sodium and water excretion.
- Constipation and other disturbances due to inadequate intake of bulk and fiber.

Intake of simple carbohydrates such as sugar should be limited. Intake of complex carbohydrates such as bread and cereals should be increased. For example, an appropriate goal in some cases might be to double the daily intake of bread and cereals, with a corresponding decrease in dietary fats and refined sugar. Carbohydrate intake should be spaced evenly throughout the day to stimulate insulin secretion.

*Fats.* Fat intake can vary greatly depending on local or family dietary habits. For example, elderly pesons who live on or near farms and regularly raise or purchase beef can consume as much as ten times more fat than suburban or city dwellers. Other farm foods such as cracklings and pickled pigs' feet, the use of lard for seasoning, and frequent servings of pork can increase the fat content of the blood to dangerous levels. Special cravings may develop for foods seasoned or cooked with fats, since flavor is enhanced. Consciously or unconsciously, many disadvantaged and chronically poor elderly people prefer fatty foods, because they satisfy hunger pains. Nevertheless, it is important to reduce fat intake to a minimum. With a low-fat diet, supplements of the fat-soluble vitamins A, D, and E should be taken.

*Vitamins.* The elderly are a high-risk group when it comes to vitamin deficiency. Contributing factors include inadequate vitamin intake, absorption disturbances, and increased vitamin requirements brought on by stress or serious illness.

Usual doses of water-soluble vitamins such as B-complex and C may be taken by the elderly without fear of toxic reaction. Excessive intake of vitamin C may cause diarrhea or watery stools and an increased potential for kidney stones.

A lifetime of poor eating habits and neglect can't be fully counterbalanced by a few weeks or months of proper nutrition in an institution, but major improvement is possible through nutritional and vitamin therapy. It's never too late to start helping a patient.

---

### Resources

Armbrecht HJ, Prendergast JM, Coe RM (eds): *Nutrition Intervention in the Aging Process.* New York, Springer-Verlag, 1984.
  Answers to questions concerning the interaction between aging and nutrition.

Natow AB, Heslin JA, Natow AJ: *Geriatric Nutrition.* New York, Van Nostrand Reinhold, 1980.
  Both a theoretical and practical information guide for proper diet maintenance for the elderly.

Roe A (ed): *Drugs and Nutrition in the Geriatric Patient.* New York, Churchill Livingstone, 1984.

# THE INSTITUTIONALIZED ELDERLY

Although only about 4 to 5 percent of the aged are institutionalized, they contribute disproportionately to certain stereotypes and constitute a large number of lives. The families of these people are deeply affected as well. How to handle Mom's or Dad's living in a nursing home is a tough emotional problem for many families.

## INSTITUTIONALIZATION SYNDROME

A great deal has been said about institutionalization and its syndrome.[1] Institutionalization may be defined as the isolation of a group of people in a confined location for the purpose of controlling their activities and separating them from society at large. Institutionalization syndrome has been identified in a number of settings. Adaptation to the institutional setting, with its confinement and regimentation, also destroys independence and initiative. The resident becomes helpless and unable to make and carry out plans. Perhaps criminal behavior or mental illness may justify this result, but aging is neither a crime nor a sickness.

An incisive study of a Massachusetts nursing home documented this phenomenon in the institutionalized elderly. The residents who learned to "play the game" and live by the institution's rules thrived; those who didn't adapt didn't survive.

Earlier observations of children in orphanages and experiments on monkeys deprived of their mothers revealed a similar passivity and helplessness. The children lagged far behind normal youngsters in their development. The monkeys failed to interact normally with other monkeys. Also, many experimental psychologists found that laboratory rats who learned complicated mazes well failed to adapt to the outside world after being released.

Sharon Curtin[2] has suggested how the custodial attitude in institutions for the elderly—the staff members' belief that old people are incapable of benefiting from treatment—contributes to institutionalization syndrome. One poignant incident she described was an attempted exchange between two old people who had been transported to the solarium of a nursing home; as they acknowledged each other and started a conversation, the nurses separated them as though this display of energy might require too much effort and shock the other residents.

Curtin describes a number of other situations in which old people were treated like children—and in some cases, bizarrely. For example, the elderly residents in one home were persuaded to don masks and "make merry as children" for a Halloween party. Curtin also suggests the reason for this custodial attitude. In many instances, old people are there to live out the rest of their lives. Although statistically this will be a number of years, neither the residents nor the staff want to accept that fact. It's as though staff members aren't clear in their own minds as to whether the nursing home is primarily a residence or a hospital. Being medically trained, they tend to resolve the conflict on the side of the hospital, with its orientation toward efficiency and restrictions. The fact that some nursing-home residents are genuinely sick may add to this orientation.

Many nursing-home administrators have complained that standard nursing training is inappropriate for workers in nursing homes where duties differ from hospitals. They point out the need for special training more appropriate to the needs of nursing home residents, although definite resistance and misinterpretation of programs that explore the values of the nursing-home system have been encountered (see Chapters 12 and 13 and Appendices 1, 2, and 3).

## WHO ARE THE INSTITUTIONALIZED ELDERLY?

About half the institutionalized elderly are diagnosed as having dementia or chronic brain syndrome (CBS), also called organic brain syndrome (OBS). CBS has four symptoms: (1) a sudden, noticeable loss of memory; (2) loss of orientation to time, places, persons, or events; (3) mental disorganization, shown by so-called word salads; and (4) emotional lability—sudden, drastic changes in mood.[3] Jarvik[4] has noted the syndrome's ambiguous nature and the strong judgmental component in its diagnosis. For instance, a depressed, mildly disorganized person with a sensory loss due to a condition like cataracts might appear to be suffering from CBS. In spite of this, however, the term chronic brain syndrome has been used casually and categorically as though it were the clearest of conditions to diagnose.

It's generally accepted that CBS has at least two causes. One is arteriosclerosis or hardening of the arteries. It's currently thought that rigidity of the smaller blood vessels in the brain is directly responsible for CBS. Transport of oxygen to the brain is diminished, and the symptoms follow. Much of the research on the effects of oxygen deficit or hypoxia, such as that described by Van Lier and Stychnie,[5] supports this idea. McFarland's[6] theory of aging is also based on the data obtained under hypobaric (low oxygen) conditions. These data are consistent with the oxygen-deficit explanation.

The other principal cause of CBS is deterioration of the brain, or senility. Neural structure, nutrients, and oxygen are necessary for proper brain functioning. Apparently a critical mass is necessary[3] for normal function. When more than that amount is destroyed, CBS or senility occurs.[3] Cross sections of brains obtained at autopsy from people who were diagnosed as having CBS indicate that their brain cells had lost their weblike structure and appeared like haystacks lined up together. The interconnections among neurons had been lost. That a critical mass may be necessary for acceptable cognitive functioning is consistent with the classic results reported by the physiological psychologist Lashley.[7] Using rats, he found it was the mass of the cerebrum rather than specific locations in it that affected the performance of typical learning and problem-solving tasks. Deficits in performance were generally proportional to the amount of cortex destroyed. When a critical mass was reached, the animals could no longer learn or solve problems.

## DEINSTITUTIONALIZATION

Because of the problems created by institutionalization, there's a movement away from it today. The recognition that mental hospitals and nursing homes can cause more problems than they solve has strongly motivated this movement.[3] The finding that many psychiatric casualties of World War II tended to live up to their "craziness" labels when, in fact, they weren't hopelessly insane, undoubtedly has also contributed to the deinstitutionalization philosphy.

Many who have worked in institutions have argued that a large percentage of the patients who are allowed or "persuaded" to leave refuse to do so; if they do leave, they waste away outside the institution and return before too much time has passed. The same workers suggest these incidents prove that disturbed people are rightfully kept confined. These arguments tend to ignore the fact that many of these patients are simply displaying the effects of the institutionalization itself—forced dependency and an inability to adapt to a self-regulated environment.[8]

In some cases, these criticisms are rationalizations by incompetent workers who are afraid of losing their jobs. The majority of nursing-home and hospital workers, however, are conscientious professionals who resent being thought of as wardens, custodians, or jailers. They feel, with some justification, that everyone in the system is treated humanely but themselves. Well-conducted training programs for workers in institutional settings emphasize the importance of their feelings. Trainers need to set good examples in their own conduct and encourage staff members to communicate with each other; staff members, in turn, should encourage residents to do the same. These are the objectives of many staff training programs and remotivation therapy, a form of group therapy for nursing-home residents and mental patients (see Chapter 13).

The advent of mood-altering drugs, such as tranquilizers and antidepressants, in the early 1950s, has helped make deinstitutionalization possible. These drugs, though perhaps over-prescribed,[9] have virtually emptied the back wards of state mental hospitals and made straitjackets and padded cells practically obsolete. It is now generally accepted that elderly and mildly disturbed people are better off in a free environment than in a custodial setting. This trend has led to widespread outpatient care and routine medication. The use of medications for old people, however, ought to be regarded as temporary; the goal of treatment should be to return to free, independent living, if at all possible.

The federal government encourages outpatient care in the community for the elderly and mildly disturbed through grants made by the National Institute of Mental Health to support paraprofessional staff for locally administered outpatient programs.[3]

In 1975, the Supreme Court provided legal backing for deinstitutionalization. It declared that residents of institutions who are not dangerous to themselves or others, who are capable of financially supporting themselves, and who are not receiving treatment, have the right to be released. Donaldson[1] has written about his personal experiences within the mental institution, and, of course, *One Flew Over the Cuckoo's Nest* has brought many injustices to the public's attention. Many patients have been released and are being released from institutions only because of their legal rights; the fact that there are so many of these people is a cogent argument that mental hospitals have sometimes acted as prisons.

Many of the staff in these hospitals have admitted informally[8] that deinstitutionalization has great merit but that it's too late for patients who have spent years in a hospital. They also state that paying patients to stay in the hospital (e.g., veteran's benefits) sabotages the movement. Finally, they feel that not enough has been done to prepare the patient and the community for release. This point has also been made by Adlestein.[10] Without family and/or community acceptance of the patient and understanding of mental illness, this movement may be seriously weakened. With community orientation, however, and programs designed to heighten public awareness to the positive aspects of deinstitutionalization, outpatient care and halfway houses may become the usual settings for treatment of mild mental disorders.

## COMMUNITY OUTPATIENT CLINICS

Psychiatrists have taken a firm stand in favor of holistic care of the aged patient. (Holistic approaches such as Goldstein's[11] emphasize treatment of the entire person.) Duke University, with the help of its psychiatry department and particularly Dr. Eric Pfeiffer, has set up a strong geriatrics and gerontology program. Dr. Maurice Linden, a classically trained psychoanalyst, has been a pioneer in this field and an aggressive advocate for the elderly. Dr. Joseph Adlestein, a psychiatrist and pioneer in the public health field, has helped start a holistically oriented medical program for the aged at Harrisburg (Pa.) Hospital that considers both medical and social problems. In the 1960s, Dr. Frank F. Furstenberg, an internist, helped set up a program oriented toward older persons' medical and social needs at Sinai Hospital in Baltimore; it has become a very effective geriatric program. Drs. Robert Butler and Elisabeth Kübler-Ross, both psychiatrists, are well know for their insights into aging.

Dr. Linden heads a medical program that is an outstanding example of an alternative to institutionalization of the elderly. His eight-point program, outlined below, works very effectively in a conservative South Philadelphia community. Its values are consistent with the community's , Dr. Linden's innovative work in psychiatry, and the movement toward deinstitutionalization.

The Jefferson Community Center, as it's called, offers eight services: treatment of (1) chronic brain syndrome, (2) acute brain syndrome, (3) malnutrition, (4) depression, and (5) psychosis, (6) education of the family and community, (7) general medical and surgical care, and (8) prevention and treatment of social breakdown syndrome.

Dr. Linden subscribes to the egalitarian value system in mental hospitals. This value system became the basis for programs funded by the National Institute of Mental Health. The egalitarian philosophy holds that (1) effective treatment requires a group contribution; (2) psychiatric treatment is an interpersonal process made up of more than electroshock, drugs, and so forth, which are threatening and impersonal; (3) all people possess insight and are potential therapists; (4) the patient's positive aspects, not the debilitating ones, should be emphasized; (5) the patient is an active participant in his or her treatment; and (6) the institutional boundaries are penetrable, and the program is part of the community. The ideal is to create a supportive and therapeutic community whose entire staff is involved in treatment of patients, under the direction of physicians.

The symptoms of CBS were discussed earlier in this chapter. *Acute brain syndrome* (ABS) has the same symptoms as CBS, but they are transient and disappear relatively shortly after onset. The major causes of ABS are cerebrovascular accidents, malnutrition, and incorrect or excessive medication. Frequently, an older person suffering an aneurysm or a temporary slowdown in the circulation of blood to the brain will display ABS. After adequate circulation has been restored, the symptoms disappear. Many stroke victims suffer a temporary, severe decrease in circulation to portions of the brain. They recover fairly quickly if there has not been severe loss of brain tissue and if blood supply is available through collateral vessels; this is true at any age.

Drug interactions are a severe problem for the elderly. Old people who "shop" from one doctor to another may get prescriptions for several different drugs to handle their emotional and physical complaints. Sometimes they take these drugs incorrectly; the drugs can accumulate or interact, causing ABS. Hospitalization may be necessary.

*Malnutrition*, a general problem in itself for the aged, is a common reason for ABS. Frequently older people forget to eat because of the lack of company and social structure in their lives. Combined with these problems may be the relative dullness of their hunger pangs as a result of general sensory losses, the difficulty of shopping for one person, trouble getting to the store, and lack of money for food. The resulting malnutrition will sometimes produce confusion and disorientation.

Linden[3] cited a study by Goldsmith that reported four to 18 percent spontaneous recovery rate among the elderly admitted to state hospitals and attributed it to the eating of decent food for a reasonable period of time. That dietary deficiencies often lead to dramatic illnesses is well known. Pellagra is due to niacin (a B-complex vitamin) deficiency. This deficiency leads to diarrhea, dermatitis, dementia, and death. The psychological symptoms are dramatic, but they disappear with proper vitamin therapy. Beriberi, a disease due to thiamin (also a B—complex vitamin) deficiency, produces a state of severe anxiety that quickly disappears with proper diet. In addition to these drastic conditions, malnutrition and lack of a balanced diet may cause general listlessness and lethargy, and probably are important contributors to slowness, confusion, or malaise observed in some aged people. Linden[3] often prescribes vitamin injections for the old as an integral part of their treatment in order to restore missing vitamins B and C. These injections also seem to increase absorption in the intestinal walls, improving nutrition.

*Depression* is one of the most common emotional problems experienced by the aged.[12,13] With the grim losses they face, this isn't surprising; however, depression can also be caused by physical disorders as well as social isolation and intrinsic psychological factors.[3] If not treated early, depression tends to worsen, and according to some authorities, it may be the start of mental illness in general. As a mildly depressed person grows older, he or she loses many psychological props, so it becomes especially necessary to give the person's emotional state prompt attention.[3]

*Psychosis* is also treated at the Jefferson Community Center. Often, it's an escape from unbearable realities the patient faces. It needs to be treated promptly because it tends to cause regression. The patient's family situation may often have contributed to the psychosis.

Parent-child conflicts may often be put on the back burner when the child marries and leaves home. When Mom or Dad comes to live with a married child, however, the same antagonisms, hostility, and bitterness start to boil up again. Dr. Virginia Hall[14] has suggested, perhaps not entirely facetiously, forming a society for the prevention of cruelty to old parents. Unhealthy parent-child interactions require that the entire family receive therapy and counseling on how to cope with each other. Often, to escape chronic guilt, the child places the parent in an institution, creating heavy guilt feelings for the child and institutionalization problems for the older person. Nursing-home personnel encounter these familial problems all the time and need to offer programs that prepare and counsel the family on how to handle their feelings. Such programs could also make it easier for the staff to handle patients.

Another important role of the Jefferson Community Center is *education of the families and the community* of its elderly clients about their own and others' aging. Guided discussions on the meaning of old age, what to expect, how to prepare for it, and how to get help are part of the program. The importance of community involvement and public understanding and acceptance of aging are essential to effective, lasting programs for the aged. Only when "you" and "I" become "we," and we are able to see ourselves as sharing the same experiences, can a dent be made in the wall of misconceptions surrounding the experience of aging. It's interesting to consider that when we concern ourselves with remedying human afflictions, we're actually talking about how we ourselves want to be treated.

General *medical and surgical disorders* make up the seventh class of problems treated at the Jefferson Community Center. Older people sometimes use physical discomforts as a pretext for going to the doctor when actually they need help with emotional problems. Many of them tend to view emotional problems as a sign of weakness, and their pride and defenses make it difficult to acknowledge psychological problems directly. The medical services not only are essential to health care but also open the door for elderly patients to air their less tangible problems.

*Social breakdown syndrome*, a typical form of alienation of the elderly from the surrounding community, is important to acknowledge and understand. The elderly may rank their various losses according to their degree of severity,[3] ranging from loss of status, to loss of personal worth, to loss of independence, to loss of mental capacity, to accepting institutionalization, and, finally, to loss of life itself. Each is a stage of deterioration of personal identity. Traditional cultures—Mexico's, for example—revere their aged and see them as positive contributors to society, thus reinforcing their sense of personal identity, whereas our culture's nontraditional attitudes tend to make them feel unwanted and unneeded. Viewing someone positively, giving love, and helping that person take the inevitable losses in stride[15] and as settling forces [16,17] can help an aged person maintain personal identity and dignity. These issues are also of primary concern at the Jefferson Community Center.

Encouraging social cooperation has been a consistent part of Linden's professional value system. His eight-point program is directed toward the whole person, and in many respects, toward the whole community. By helping and sharing with each other, its members can also help themselves.

## ADULT DAY CARE

Until recently, the traditional approach to the treatment and care of chronic illness among the elderly focused primarily on institutionalization as a long-term-care solution. The adult day-care center, a *day* program for impaired adults in a group setting away from home, now represents a viable alternative for many elderly. Centers provide activities that encourage the elderly to maintain their own level of physical well-being and promote a renewed interest in life through various social, emotional, and psychological support services.

The care provided by health professionals in a day-care center is not a substitute for 24-hour institutionalized care. But it is an excellent alternative for those elderly who do not require full-time care. Adult day care is part of a long-term-care continuum blending psychosocial and health services. Older citizens prefer to remain in their own communities, and when given the option, prefer adult or elderly day-care facilities to institutionalization. Adult day care addresses needs not always provided in long-term-care facilities and at a tremendous savings.

There are many kinds of day-care programs. Some are community-based, while others are sponsored by nursing homes. Broadly speaking, adult day-care programs can include senior citizen centers, congregate meal sites, friendly visitors programs, home health care, neighborhood health centers, and foster care. There is no one ideal model or blueprint for a successful adult day-care program; each type of program offers special or unique services.

Depending upon the extent of staff and facilities, a program may include medical, nutritional, and nursing service, restorative therapies (physical, occupational, speech, art, music), clerical, recreational and social service, and transportation.

Most centers have an advisory board of concerned citizens or community leaders. An interdisciplinary team approach is highly recommended in coordinating services. This usually means direct planning, implementation, and evaluation by a team of professionals including a social worker, nurses, physicians, a nutritionist, therapists, and the client's family and personal physician.

## NURSING HOMES

The elderly person who requires institutionalization is generally being treated for a catastrophic illness. The illness may be a heart attack, cerebrovascular accident, broken hip, or similar problem that necessitates admission to an acute-care setting. The patient may be physically ill and also suffer from a dementia or dementing illness. Dementia is a disease affecting the mental state of the patient as discussed in Chapter 4. Often the primary diagnosis becomes so complex that continued care is required at a nursing home or convalescent center.

Skilled nursing homes certified by Medicare provide 24-hour care to those persons who need special services provided by registered or licensed practical nurses. A skilled facility also offers rehabilitative services. Usually, a person seeking skilled services will have been recently discharged from a hospital for short-term care to nursing homes. The coverage of these skilled services will usually be covered under Medicare. Patients suffering from a dementia are generally considered to require custodial care.

Convalescent homes may provide many of the same services as a skilled-care nursing home but at a lower level of skill. Of the approximately 23,000 nursing homes throughout the United States, less than 23 percent are actually skilled-care nursing facilities.

## RETIREMENT COMMUNITIES AND CONDOS

Retirement communities and condominiums for senior citizens are not limited to the booming sun belt states where many elderly folks move to enjoy the sunshine and moderate climates. Retirement complexes, condominiums, and apartment projects exclusively for the elderly who are able to live independently are rapidly becoming popular living options. Like Westminster Village in Allentown, Pa., many retirement complexes are associated with or part of a nursing-home facility. In many retirement villages, routine and/or emergency nursing services are provided.

## SHELTERED HOMES

For those elderly who need minimal care or supervision but who still desire to live in a noninstitutional environment, the sheltered home or share-a-home is another option. There are usually private or semiprivate rooms with a common dining area, where fellowship and warm conversation abound. Church-affiliated share-a-home programs are becoming more popular. Few states have established strict laws or guidelines governing the sheltered-home arrangement, and persons seeking this less expensive option must be careful in selecting a home.

---

**References**
1. Donaldson G: *Insanity Inside Out*. New York, Crown, 1976.
2. Curtin S: *Nobody Ever Died of Old Age*. Boston, Little, Brown, 1972.
3. Linden M: Paper presented at Continuing Education Conference on Society and the Aging at Harrisburg Area Community College, Harrisburg, Pa., 1974.
4. Jarvik L: Paper presented at Continuing Education Conference on Psychodynamics of Aging at New York University Postgraduate Center for Mental Health, New York, 1976.
5. Van Lier E, Stychnie J (eds): *Hypoxia*. Chicago, University of Chicago Press, 1963.
6. McFarland R, in Van Lier E, Stychnie J (eds): *Hypoxia*. Chicago, University of Chicago Press, 1963.
7. Lashley KS: *Brain Mechanisms and Intelligence*. Chicago, University of Chicago Press, 1929.
8. Fleishman J, McKenna C: Unpublished study, 1975.
9. Whittaker J, Fleishman J: Biological foundations of psychology: Behavior and states of awareness, in *Introduction to Psychology*, ed 3. Philadelphia, Saunders, 1976.
10. Adlestein J: Personal communication, 1976.
11. Goldstein K: Concerning rigidity. *Character and Personality*, 1943; 11:209.

12. Blum J: Paper presented at Continuing Education Conference on Psychodynamics of Aging at New York University Postgraduate Center for Mental Health, New York, 1976.

13. Busse E, Pfeiffer E (eds): *Behavior and Adaptation in Late Life*. Boston, Little, Brown, 1969.

14. Hall V: Personal communication, 1976.

15. Taylor C: Paper presented at Continuing Education Conference on Society and the Aging at Harrisburg Area Community College, Harrisburg, Pa., 1974.

16. Pollack O, Paper presented at S.I.E.C.U.S. Conference, Philadelphia, 1973.

17. Pollack O: Paper presented at Continuing Education Conference on Psychodynamics of Aging at New York University Postgraduate Center for Mental Health, New York, 1976.

**Resources**

Bowker LH: *Humanizing Institutions for the Aged*. Lexington, Ma., Lexington Books, 1982.

Brickner PW, Scharer LK, Conanan B, et al: *Health Care of Homeless People*. New York, Springer Publishing Co, 1984.

Conger SA, Moore KD: *Social Work in the Long-Term Care Facility*. New York, Van Nostrand Reinhold, 1981.

Coward RT, Lee GR: *The Elderly in Rural Society*. New York, Springer Publishing Co, 1984.

State-of-the-art overview of the situation of America's elderly population in rural areas, including their special problems, handicaps, needs, and present level of services.

Ham RJ (ed): *Geriatric Medicine Annual: 1986*. Oradell, NJ, Medical Economics Books, 1986.

Annual includes articles on antidepressant therapy, incontinence, systolic hypertension, estrogen use, surgical diagnosis, abuse of the elderly, adverse drug reactions, falls, thyroid disease, movement disorders, new treatment methods in cardiology, and sexual dysfunction.

Ham RJ, Holtzman JM, Marcy ML, et al: *Primary Care Geriatrics: A Case-based Learning Program*. Boston, John Wright-PSG, Inc, 1983.

An individualized learning manual for training health-care professionals including nurses, nurse practitioners, and physician assistants. An excellent step-by-step instructional guide. Pre- and post-tests are included for each chapter, and an extensive annotated bibliographical section provides follow-up readings and media resources. A must reference for nursing homes and geriatric centers. Prepared under the auspices of The American Geriatrics Society.

Kapp HT, Bigot A: *Geriatrics and the Law.* New York, Springer Publishing Co, 1985.

Examines aspects of geriatrics practice from a legal viewpoint, explaining complex medical-legal issues in a clear and concise manner.

Lawton MP, Hoover SL: *Community Housing Choices for Older Americans.* New York, Springer Publishing Co, 1981.

Focuses on the housing problems of the vast majority of the elderly who live in their own homes in ordinary communities.

McDowell FH (ed): *Choosing a Nursing Home for the Person with Intellectual Loss.* White Plains, NY, Burke Rehabilitation Center, 1980.

A brief information booklet for families. Available from the Burke Rehabilitation Center, 785 Mamaroneck Ave, White Plains, NY, 10605.

Monk A (ed): *Handbook of Gerontological Services.* New York, Van Nostrand Reinhold, 1985.

O'Brien CL: *Adult Daycare: A Practical Guide.* Monterey, CA, Wadsworth Health Sciences Division, 182.

A rationale for day-care centers for the elderly. The presentation of various models and resources for starting a center is outlined.

Rich T, Gilmore A: *Basic Concepts of Aging—A Programmed Manual.* Washington, D.C., U.S. Government Printing Office, 1972.

Schneider EL (ed): *The Teaching Nursing Home: A New Approach to Geriatric Research, Education, and Clinical Care.* New York, Raven Press, 1984.

A look at innovative ways of joining the forces of the academic medical community and long-term care institutions.

Spicker SF, Ingman SR: *Vitalizing Long-term Care: The Teaching Nursing Home and Other Perspectives.* New York, Springer Publishing Co, 1984.

Among the topics covered are the theoretical and policy implications for care of the aged, medical training in nursing homes, quality-of-life approaches to long-term care, and advocacy design in institutional planning.

Williams RF (ed): *Rehabilitation in the Aging.* New York, Raven Press, 1984.

Named 1984 book of the year in gerontology by the *American Journal of Nursing*, it reflects a comprehensive, integrated approach to the medical and rehabilitative management of geriatric patients.

# 9

# SEXUALITY

Sex, one of our strongest drives, isn't discussed openly at any age. Privately, we seek insight into the role sex plays in our lives, and any reasonably good book on the subject is bound to make the best-seller lists. Our general ignorance of sexuality is especially acute when it comes to telling the elderly how to behave sexually. In effect, we deny their desire and ability to keep on practicing what they've enjoyed most of their adult lives.

Why do we expect people to lose their sexual drive as they grow older? The "dirty old man" image implies that lust, desire, and the willingness to share love are perversions in the elderly. The many jokes about older people and sex may also reflect fears about our own sexual performance; perhaps they're a way of rationalizing a lackluster episode as a result of "getting old."

These expectations imply that we still view sex as an obligation. Maybe older people, whose reproductive years are over, are seen as glad to give it up. Or perhaps we feel that because aging often brings impaired health it follows that it also impairs sexuality.

## WHAT IS SEXUALITY?

Sexuality is a special kind of communication between people that involves physical contact and pleasurable psychological arousal. It's a direct way of expressing strong affection and love. A frequent misconception about sexuality is that it's the same as coitus. Any definition that views coitus as necessary to human sexuality overemphasizes the physical sex act. Coitus can, of course, result in conception, and a man and woman may want to express their love for each other by having a baby. But any definition that views conception as the purpose of sex is narrow and moralistic. It clearly would suggest that any person who is no longer fertile need not even consider the act of sexual intercourse. This is absurd! Touching, expressing love, physical and psychological arousal, and coitus are all parts of sexuality. We don't expect an elderly couple to stop loving each other; there's no reason to expect them to stop expressing that love sexually.

## SEXUAL NORMS FOR THE AGED

Pfeiffer[1] reported an extensive study that explored the sexual attitudes and activities of the aged. Interestingly, the people interviewed liked talking about their sexuality. However, the young professionals who interviewed them reported feeling uncomfortable asking older people questions about sex. The adult children of the aged were very concerned that the study intruded into their parents' privacy and also expressed personal embarrassment.

Two hundred fifty people, including 31 married couples, were interviewed. In checking the reliability of their answers, it was found that spouses independently agreed with each other 90 percent of the time.

The results showed that sex plays an important role in the lives of people in their 60s, 70s, 80s, and 90s. Of men in their late 60s, it was found that:
- 80 percent were interested in sex
- 50 percent participated regularly (on the average of once a week or more)

Ten years later, in the same group:
- 25 percent were still sexually active on a regular basis
- Some decreased the frequency of their sexual activity, some stayed the same, and a few increased their frequency

For women in their late 60s, it was found that:

- 50 percent had continued interest in sex
- 30 percent were sexually active on a regular basis

Ten years later, of the same women:

- 30 percent had continued sexual interest
- 20 percent still enjoyed sex regularly

When the men were asked why they stopped having sex, they blamed themselves. When the married women were asked why they stopped, "It was him" was the frequent answer. Generally, the man stopped the sex in a marriage. For unmarried women, stopping was blamed on lack of a partner.

There were other interesting findings:

- Sexual experience early in life is related to sexual activity in old age; those who had strong interest in sex during their early years remained interested
- It's not true that "you can wear 'it' out"
- Physical health is related to sexuality in old age
- For men, marital status made no difference in sexual activity
- Only married women reported an active sex life

Women outlive men by an average of eight years, and thus are subject to approximately 12 years of widowhood (men are four years older than their spouses on the average). Maggie Kuhn,[2] head of the Gray Panthers, has offered a cogent argument for marriage between older women and younger men based on these statistics. Widowers have an ample field to play, while widows do not. The frequent cry from older women, "A good man is hard to find," is thus a realistic complaint.

## PHYSICAL ASPECTS

The same study[1] also showed that where impotence existed, very little of it was due to organic causes. Sexuality still remained strongly a matter of state of mind. Because it's more difficult to become aroused as sensory sensitivity decreases with advancing age, touching assumes more importance as a sexual expression. Once sexual arousal occurs, however, it tends to last longer. Sexual pleasure is the same for the old as for the young.[3]

## HOW SOCIAL ATTITUDES CAN HELP

We often treat the elderly very foolishly as far as sexuality is concerned. We tend to be insensitive to their needs and discourage remarriage even though remarriage may be an excellent idea. Sexual relations between old people seem to embarrass their children and spark conflicts and disbelief about their physical relationship that go back to adolescence. "Other people's parents make love—but *mine?*" This sentiment seems to linger far beyond childhood.

Because our society doesn't acknowledge that sex can be an important part of later life, old people with sex problems tend to encounter indifference, disbelief, or scorn when they ask for help.[4] Doctors are sometimes the worst offenders. One pragmatic and understanding housing manager of an apartment complex for the aged is said to encourage the tenants to keep up their love lives by approving their expressions of mutual interest and, when possible, even arranging for adjacent apartments when a liaison seems likely to last. This natural, casual attitude keeps morale high.

---

**References**

1. Pfeiffer E: Paper presented at S.I.E.C.U.S. Conference, Philadelphia, 1973.

2. Kuhn M: Paper presented at S.I.E.C.U.S. Conference, Philadelphia, 1973.

3. Ham RJ: Sexual dysfunction in the elderly, in *Geriatric Medicine Annual: 1986*. Oradell, NJ, Medical Economics Books, 1986.

4. Lief A: Paper presented at S.I.E.C.U.S. Conference, Philadelphia, 1973.

# 10

# DEALING WITH DEATH

## SOCIAL ATTITUDES TOWARD DEATH

Our society makes strenuous efforts to protect its young from contact with death. As we enter our middle years, we seem to awaken to the possibility of our own death.[1] We're more likely to know someone facing death and even more likely to know someone who's mourning a dead relative. Our early protection from death, while well intended, leaves us exceptionally vulnerable to emotional shock when we do encounter it. We have to learn all at once how to cope with the anticipated loss of our own life or that of a loved one. We suddenly become aware that the reality of death is very remote from the idealized and perhaps religious or euphemistic conceptions of it that we were taught as children. The price that has to be paid for this ignorance is emotionally draining, but dealing with death helps complete our maturity. Because our society is secretive about death, there's a lack of useful knowledge on the subject.

## DEATH AS A PART OF LIFE

There's one fate all human beings have in common—death, dying, losing oneself, and the awareness of it. Arthur Koestler has spoken of the uniqueness and delicate nature of that awareness. The ability to anticipate our own death and reflect on it distinguishes us from all other species. We may wonder whether there will be a world without us; Linden [2] has pointed out the egocentricity intrinsic to our thoughts on our own death.

Death provides the background against which all life occurs. The greatest risk of living is the ultimate mistake—to cause one's own death. Most theories regarding death focus on our vulnerability to the thought of it and how our perception of death helps shape personality. Although open discussion of dying has been rare in this society, there's convincing evidence of our omnipresent concern with it. It's hard to think of a religion without a view on death.

For the aged, death becomes a very close, real consideration. As friends and relatives of the same generation die, the elderly tend to take a pragmatic interest in funerals, cemeteries, wills, and estates. This interest isn't morbid, but reflects an acknowledgment that death is inevitable.

## DYING WITH DIGNITY

Dying with dignity is of greater concern to the elderly than the simple realization that death is inevitable. The awareness that one may lose contol of bodily functions is especially frightening. For example, an 87-year-old woman living in a nursing home had hardening of the arteries and chronic brain syndrome. Frequently she acted paranoid, accusing people of harming her. Part of her paranoia probably came from loss of sight and hearing. She had lost sphincter control, had to rely on others to move her, and had special religious dietary needs the nursing home couldn't meet. There was no hope of cure. She had already cut her social ties and could never return to her home. This woman told her daughter how miserable and undignified she felt: "That life has come to this! I'd rather be dead."

Heifetz and Mangel[3] have written extensively about the patient's right to die with dignity. They even suggest it's the physician's responsibility to prevent the indignities of biological vegetation and emotional and financial drain it imposes on the family. The ethics they espouse warrant some serious thought. They share with the reader the human emotional component of dying as well as the biological aspects. They also describe hospices—places where dying people receive sympathetic care without an attempt to prolong their lives (see section on hospices).

## HOW THE ELDERLY APPROACH DEATH

Elisabeth Kübler-Ross has achieved great acclaim for her studies on how people face death, one aspect of the field of thanatology. Her work contains profound insights. What occurs when people face death is actually quite different from what we might expect. Perhaps more than anything else, dying people don't want to be left alone or made to feel useless in this last confrontation of their lives. Kübler-Ross sums up: "This is perhaps the greatest lesson we learned from our patients. LIVE, so you do not have to look back and say: 'God, how I have wasted my life.'"[4]

The one point she emphasizes over all others, however, is that it's never too late while alive to share feelings, communicate with others, and overcome isolation and loneliness—the essentials of human growth. She illustrates this idea in the following touching passage that describes the reactions of the dying patients to being asked to share their innermost feelings in a seminar on dying:

> The patients who were asked to serve were no problem either. They were often quite grateful to be "useful," to feel that someone needed them rather than the other way around. When we started to talk they quickly overcame their initial shyness and rather quickly shared with us the fantastic loneliness they felt. Strangers whom we had never met shared their grief, their isolation, their inability to talk about their illness and death with their next-of-kin. They expressed their anger at the physician who did not "level" with them, at the minister who tried to console them with the too often repeated phrase "It is God's will," or at friends and relatives who visited them with the inevitable "Cheer up, it's not so bad." We learned to identify quickly with them and became much more sensitive to their needs and fears than ever before. They taught us a great deal about living and dying, and they appreciated our asking them to be our teachers.[4]

In a particularly poignant anecdote, Kübler-Ross describes the effects of the teaching seminar on a social worker at the hospital who had been working with the family of a dying patient. The social worker reflected on the changes she experienced as a result of discussing death:

> I had a similar problem in working with many aged and infirm clients in the past years. I always felt that old age and sickness was so devastating, that although I wanted to communicate hope to them, I only communicated despair. I think that the seminar has helped me to see that life did not have to end in mental and physical agony.[4]

In reflecting upon what was learned in counseling the dying patients, the same worker continued: "In working with any patient, there must be a goal toward which you both are striving and some belief that movement to resolution or comfort is possible. It seems to me from observations of the interviews that listening is a comfort to these patients." In recalling a dying man who was unable to convey to his wife the loneliness and other feelings he was experiencing, the social worker added:

> I think another great help a social worker can give is to the family of the dying patient—not so much in the way stressed by so much of the casework literature (homemaker, financial aid, etc.) but in helping them to relate better to the patient. Mr. N. wanted to talk about his illness to his wife and she to him. But they were each afraid to cause the other pain and did not know how much the other knew. With reassurance from the staff, Mrs. N. was able to broach the subject with her husband and they were then able to share and to be a source of comfort to each other—instead of suffering alone.[4]

More recently Kübler-Ross[5] has noted that her work with dying people has led to some interesting cross-cultural findings concerning the memories of patients who were revived after being diagnosed as clinically dead. This has stirred up quite a controversy.

## DEATH IN AN INSTITUTIONAL SETTING

Since many dying people are in hospitals or nursing homes, it becomes the doctor's job to handle their approach to death. In many respects this is the poorest choice.[4] Doctors have as much trouble as anyone in coping with death, perhaps more so because of their commitment to fighting it. Because they regard death as a personal defeat, many doctors may be unable to share with patients the emotions involved in openly facing death.

Being in an institution can compound the dying patient's problems. The institution is restrictive and regimented; it's emotionally sterile and lacks the vitality found in places where healthy people are free to make decisions and mistakes. It's no wonder so many terminal patients want to go home to die. Along with others, Kübler-Ross has made it evident that we need to talk more openly about death with dying patients and to stop overprotecting them from knowledge of their condition.

## HOSPICES*

For terminally ill patients who prefer an alternative to traditional hospital care, there is a rapidly growing concept sweeping the nation—hospice. Hospice is an old word with a new meaning. The old word refers to a medieval way station where a weary pilgrim could stop for refreshments during a long journey. The new birth of the word implies "living until we die." This is encouraged by using highly specialized health-care techniques emphasizing the management of pain and other symptoms associated with terminal illness. The hospice concept provides care and concern for the patient, family, and close friends. The hospice-care team includes physicians, nurses, social workers, clergymen, allied health-care providers, and specially trained volunteers.

The hospice concept can be implemented in a hospital setting, nursing or convalescent center, hospice facility, or in the comfort of the patient's own home or apartment—which ap-

---

*Much of this material is from Kohut and Kohut, *Hospice: Caring for the Terminally Ill*. See References.

pears to be the most feasible and satisfying situation for most dying patients.

The hospice movement is gaining popularity throughout the United States. Hospice provides a humanistic manner of dealing with terminally ill patients and their families and friends. It also provides an alternative to the enormous costs usually associated with short- and long-term care of dying patients in traditional health-care environments.

The first hospice program in the United States was the Connecticut Hospice of New Haven. It was established in 1970 as a demonstration project supported by the National Cancer Institute. Initially, it offered only home-care services, but today it is a free standing independent 44-bed hospice facility in Branford, Connecticut. The medical director for the Connecticut Hospice, Dr. Sylvia Lack, was formally on staff at St. Christopher's Hospice in London. The inpatient program has not supplanted the home-care service, for it admits only those persons who can no longer be adequately cared for at home by their families.

The Connecticut Hospice served as a springboard for the formation of a National Hospice Organization (NHO) founded in 1978. NHO is nonprofit and incorporated with headquarters near Washington, D.C. It is dedicated to promoting and maintaining quality hospice care for the terminally ill and ongoing support for their families.

NHO is actively engaged in communicating areas of concern to established and newly organized hospices throughout the country. Issues include standards criteria, education and training, research and evaluation, reimbursement and licensure legislation, professional liaison, ethics, and public relations. The ultimate goal of NHO is to totally integrate hospice care into the entire spectrum of the American health care system.

NHO has a full-time staff of ten and a cadre of volunteers. Information concerning NHO is available from the headquarters:

National Hospice Organization
1901 N. Fort Myer Drive, Suite 402
Arlington, Virginia 22209
Phone: (703) 243-5900

Hospice programs exist in all states and most are affiliated with NHO. There are individual, institutional, cooperative, and provider memberships, in addition to recognized state affiliates.

In implementing the hospice concept, three main goals are:
- To ease the physical discomfort of the terminally ill patient by employing pharmaceutical and advanced clinical techniques for effective symptom control.
- To ease the psychological discomfort of the terminally ill patient through programs allowing for active participation in scheduled activities or periods of peaceful withdrawal as determined by the patient.
- To aid in maintaining the emotional equilibrium of the patient and the family as they go through the traumatic life experience of progressive disease and ultimately the final separation of death.

Volunteer training is an integral part of the hospice program. The volunteer, selected from the community, becomes a part of the health-care team and identifies with an individual patient. The volunteer works with the patient and family giving support, running errands, easing burdens, and remains during the period of bereavement.

The hospice concept views death as a natural process of life. It is a humane and peaceful method of treatment for the dying and their families.

In approximately 40 percent of the cases, the most common reason for admission to a hospice is the need to give respite to relatives who are care-givers for a dying person. About 20 percent of the admissions are social isolates with no family or friends willing or able to care for them, and 60 percent of the admissions need help with better control of their pain. Thus, hospice inpatients represent a mix of social and/or clinical needs. The hospice program, therefore, is not just a program that purports to care for the terminally ill. It is a program for meeting a wide range of physical, social, psychological, and spiritual needs. It is a program of health-care delivery, consisting of clearly identifiable components.

- Hospice is a *humane* way of caring for dying patients and their families.

and family *need* and is not denied because of inability to pay.

- The patient's *comfort* is the primary goal with an emphasis on *pain* and *symptom control.*
- The patient, family, and other persons essential to the patient's care comprise the *unit of care.* The hospice patient's "family" refers to the patient's immediate relatives including spouse, siblings, children, and parents. Additionally, other relatives and persons with close personal ties may be designated as members of the unit of care by mutual agreement among the patient, individual(s), and hospice staff.
- Care is provided primarily in the patient's home, but when available, hospice *inpatient* and *outpatient* facilities supplement *home care* services. Inpatient and home care services are closely integrated to insure continuity and coordination with home care.
- Hospice identifies and coordinates appropriate *community services* to provide complete care of the patient and family.
- Care is available *seven days a week, 24 hours a day.*
- A medically supervised *interdisciplinary* team of professionals and volunteers plans and provides the necessary care. The hospice physician directs the overall medical aspects of the program. The patient/family's own physician is a member of the care team and remains the primary physician.
- Trained *volunteers* are an integral part of the interdisciplinary team, supplementing and complementing the team's efforts. Volunteers engage in a wide array of services including housekeeping chores and transportation.
- Hospice provides professional *bereavement* care and support for the family often up to and even beyond a year after the patient's death.
- *Education, training,* and *evaluation* are ongoing activities in the program. Education involves educating the patient, family, and interdisciplinary team on the topic of death and dying; and educating the family in procedures and techniques for caring for the patient in the home.
- Development or formal *fundraising* activities are often part of the managerial and/or fiscal dimension of the hospice program.

It must be understood and cautioned that *not* all hospice

programs incorporate all of the components identified herein. For illustration, some are entirely home-care oriented, while others are exclusively institutional or hospital-based units, others provide no home service or limited or no bereavement counseling. Many operate on an around-the-clock basis, while other programs have limited hours. There is no prototype or model blue print for a successful hospice.

Inpatient hospices are alternatives to the majority of facilities now accommodating most terminally ill patients, that is, patients who will eventually die in a hospital or nursing home. Although there are commonalities among the different types of hospices—*inpatient, outpatient, home care*—there are distinct differences due primarily to the philosophy held rather than the architecture or physical plant of the facilities.

---

### References

1. Pollack O: Paper presented at S.I.E.C.U.S. Conference, Philadelphia, 1973.

2. Linden M: Personal communication, 1976.

3. Heifetz MD, Mangel C: *The Right to Die.* New York, Berkley Publishing Co, 1976.

4. Kübler-Ross E: *The Final Stage of Growth.* New York, Spectrum Books, 1976.

5. Kübler-Ross E: In her own words. *People* 1976; 24(Nov.):66.

6. Kohut JM, Kohut S: *Hospice: Caring for the Terminally Ill.* Springfield, IL, Charles C. Thomas Publisher, 1985.

7. Kohut S: *Occupational Therapy: Its Definition and Functions.* Rockville, MD, American Occupational Association, 1969.

### Resources

Goodman LM: *Death and the Creative Life.* New York, Springer Publishing Co, 1981.

Kastenbaum R (ed): *Between Life and Death.* New York, Springer Publishing Co, 1979.

Kohut JM, Kohut S: *Hospice: Caring for the Terminally Ill.* Springfield, IL, Charles C. Thomas Publishers, 1985.
    Written by the authors, this book provides an easy reference for persons who want to establish, maintain, or participate in a hospice program. Physicians, nurses, therapists, social and human service workers, and hospital and public health administrators will find valuable informa-

and hospital and public health administrators will find valuable information included in its 11 chapters and extensive appendices. The book is ideal for training hospice volunteers and staff, and represents an excellent source for any person interested in the hospice concept in hospitals, nursing homes, or community-based settings. Chapters address issues and topics such as death and dying, cancer patients, volunteer staff training, support systems, excerpts from volunteer's diaries, pain control, terminally ill children, grief and bereavement, stress management, and ethical and legal issues.

Lonetto R: *Children's Conceptions of Death.* New York, Springer Publishing Co, 1980.

Maikel WM, Sinon V: *The Hospice Concept.* New York, American Cancer Society, 1978.

Perrallay L, Mallica M: Public knowledge of hospice care. *Nursing Outlook,* 1981; Jan.:46.

Worden JW: *Grief Counseling and Grief Therapy: A Handbook for the Mental Health Practitioner.* New York, Springer Publishing Co, 1982.

# PART 2

---

# TREATMENT MODALITIES

# 11

# BRIDGING THE GAP BETWEEN THEORY AND PRACTICE

The preceding chapters have described the challenges confronting the elderly and what happens during the aging process. The sociological and psychological aspects of aging and the physical changes and special needs of old people have been highlighted and spelled out.

Gerontologists and geriatric medical and social-service workers are helping awaken the public conscience to the problems of aging, and are introducing new ideas, refreshing attitudes, and even new terminology. Applying research findings and new training techniques to improve life for the aged should be a national priority. The establishment of the National Institute on Aging (NIA) is a monumental step toward enhancing the quality of life for the elderly through the funding of scientific investigations. While it's important to understand and disseminate theoretical and interdisciplinary discoveries that can result in better care for the elderly, it's necessary first to shatter the many myths and stereotypes associated with the aged and the process of growing old. With the rapidly developing theoretical interest in the elderly, there must be a corresponding practical application of new techniques that benefit both the institutionalized and the home-bound elderly. A bridge must be built to connect the theoretical with the practical and clinical if the quality of everyday life for the elderly is to be significantly improved. This can be done not only in hospitals and nursing homes but also in the many innovative programs—home health care, day care, senior citizens' centers, outreach clinics, Meals on Wheels, and congregate feeding—that have been developed to assist the elderly in many communities.

When an elderly person enters an institution, the orientation or intake process begins with a comprehensive assessment of his or her capabilities—physical, psychological, social, cognitive, and functional. A relocation therapy program makes the move from a familiar home to the health-care facility easier. A psychological condition called transfer trauma is likely to occur when the elderly, especially if they're confused, are moved from one home to another, or even from one floor to another in the same nursing home. The result of transfer trauma is serious illness. It's shocking but true that 65 percent of all American elderly moved from one nursing home to another die within six months.[1] Therefore, relocation therapy is often a prerequisite for survival.

A program of reality orientation (Chapter 12) or remotivation therapy (Chapter 13) may be warranted for the bewildered institutionalized man or woman. Many facilities provide additional social, psychological, and physical incentives like music, occupational, vocational, recreational, physical, and psychosocial therapy. Counseling patients on death and dying and pre- and post-retirement and legal rights seminars and workshops are becoming standard and even mandatory offerings in some health-care facilities.

Therapy, modality, and practical treatment programs must be born out of an understanding derived from scientific conclusions about the aging process. Chapter 8 gives a scientific definition of chronic or organic brain syndrome (CBS). Someone who suffers from CBS needs help, not pity. Reality orientation (RO) is a systematic program for helping badly confused people. For many of them, such a program can restore a rich and productive life. Reorientation is the first step in the psychological rehabilitation of the confused, disoriented patient. There's a direct correlation between patients' ability to function adequately in their environment and their degree of orientation to that environment. RO provides a special awareness and a struc-

tured course of action for all members of the health-care team—
nurses, physicians, nurse's aides, occupational and physical
therapists, orderlies, food-service workers, volunteers, relatives, and friends. In today's world of educational and medical
acountability, RO is increasingly being required by federal,
state, county, and municipal agencies, and endorsed by professional accreditation associations for inclusion during preservice
and inservice training of medical and nonprofessional support
personnel. This educational program of improved communication includes staff training in nursing homes, hospitals, institutions for the mentally retarded, and other short- and long-term-
care facilities.

"We believe that the ultimate test of our research and training programs is the difference they make in the quality of life of
older people," says Dr. George L. Maddox, director of the Center for the Study of Aging and Human Development at Duke
University. The following chapter, in the spirit of that state-
ment, provides practical guidelines for the use of an RO program, whether it's in a private home, hospital, or other health-
care facility. We're all growing older. The ultimate goal is a rich
and happy life regardless of our age or circumstances. This, of
course, takes communication among family and friends of the
patient or resident and the health-care staff.

---

### References
1. *Nursing Home Relocation Team.* Commonwealth of Pennsylvania, Department of Public Welfare, Camp Hill, PA, 1976.

### Resources
Burnside I: *Working with the Elderly: Group Process and Techniques*, ed 2. Bel-
   mont, CA, Wadsworth Health Sciences Division, 1984.
   The book does not teach the reader about group dynamics; its purpose
   is to delineate the modifications and special types of groups appropriate
   for work with older clients or patients. It includes 19 chapters with contributions from specialists representing many disciplines.

Ernst NS, West HL: *Nursing Home Staff Deveolpment: A Guide for Inservice Programs.* New York, Springer Publishing Co, 1983.

# 12

# REALITY ORIENTATION

Reality orientation is not reality therapy in a historical or even clinical sense. It is not a watered-down version of Harris's *I'm OK—You're OK*. It is not strictly a program for the elderly, but benefits both young and old. It provides a special awareness and structured course of action for all members of the health-care team.

Reality orientation is built on the premise that an individual's ability to function adequately in his or her environment is directly correlated with the degree of orientation to that environment. From facts such as date, time, place, and similar environmental clues, an individual constructs a basic framework from which the more complex patterns of behavior and daily routines develop. When someone is no longer exposed to positive, meaningful stimuli from which to extract environmental clues, he or she may start to lose the ability to construct this framework. This lack of exposure, whether caused by personal limitations or social isolation, results in inappropriate, inadequate, or confused behavior. Such a person may forget where he or she is, who the surrounding people are, and what's expected in a given situation.

Reality orientation directly addresses the problems of confused, disoriented behavior and memory loss associated with lack of social interaction and positive stimuli. When using this technique, health-care personnel actively and repetitively present orientation information to an individual whenever he or she seems confused or disoriented. This process gives the confused person the information needed to begin reconstructing the environmental framework. Once the patient starts to relocate himself or herself in time and place, it's hoped that the inappropriate behavioral patterns will begin to change for the better and eventually disappear.

The RO program is also designed for the family and friends of confused persons living at home or in a long-term-care facility. With an understanding of RO and their role in it, family and friends can join the health-care team in assisting the confused person.

## ASSESSING THE ELDERLY PATIENT

Unfortunately, many old people who appear confused are automatically labeled "senile" or "uncooperative" and the underlying cause of their behavior isn't investigated.

Confused behavior may reflect a functional disorder—that is, a disturbance of mental functioning that occurs without physiological changes in the brain. Under psychiatric care, many older patients with functional disorders have significantly restored their normal patterns of thought, speech, and physical activity.

On the other hand, confused behavior may result from an organic disorder associated with physiological changes that produce brain dysfunction or damage, as previously described in Chapter 8. Confused behavior may also result from both an organic and a functional disorder. It's almost always compounded by changes in physical environment, as when a person is hospitalized or relocated. Other contributing factors include sensory or perceptual alterations, previous behavior patterns, loss of status or independence, and the attitudes of others.

As mentioned in Chapter 8, physiological changes in the brain that produce confused or bizarre behavior may be chronic or organic, or they may be acute or of short duration. Acute brain syndrome (ABS) can be reversed by correcting the condition that caused it—malnutrition, for example. CBS, however, is essentially irreversible, since it results from hardening of the arteries supplying brain and/or from deterioration of the brain tissue itself.

Although chronic brain syndromes are irreversible, under certain circumstances considerable improvement is possible in the person's relationships with others, personal habits, and daily activities. Thorough investigation into the cause of the confusion is needed to determine the proper handling of the confused geriatric patient.

Once the cause or causes are determined, it's the responsibility of those working or living with a confused individual to bring that person back to reality. The process may be a long and tedious one, but as long as there are no signs of regression, progress is being made.

Confusion—what is it? Its symptoms can be frighteningly severe. They vary from person to person and include forgetfulness, drastic mood changes, agitation, repeated inappropriate behavior, impaired judgment and intellect, and changes in orientation to person, place, and time. Nearly every elderly patient entering a nursing home exhibits a certain amount of confusion. The separation from family and friends and the changes in environment, living habits, diet, and sleeping patterns all contribute to disorientation and depression. Separation from home and family may also cause extreme anxiety. This kind of confusion can—and should—be remedied. (Refer to Chapter 5.)

Tension and anxiety further unhinge the already confused resident. Your goal is to relax and reorient the patient. Most confused elderly people know they're confused—that's one reason they're so upset. They want help. If you deny their condition, you deny them help. That's why it's important to be truthful with confused persons. They can sense deception and insincerity. Once you've acknowledged their mental state, you can assess its severity and start taking constructive measures to deal with it.

Not too long ago, confused patients were dealt with by dumping them in back wards where they experienced no mental stimulation and so continued to deteriorate ever faster. Today, we deal with confused geriatric patients truthfully and realistically. Mental faculties dim when people are left without daily conversation concerning current events, weather, holidays, and the concerns of living. It's the purpose of RO to reorient people as much as possible, and at the very least, to stop any further deterioration.

Begin by assessing the patient. Included in this chapter are two pre-RO tests to determine the degree of confusion and helplessness. When giving the tests, treat the patient courteously. The questions you must ask may cause feelings of inadequacy, even embarrassment. Hurrying the patient along will cause more anxiety and confusion. Let the patient take his or her time. If necessary, restate the question gently and tactfully. A calm, friendly, respectful manner will help put the patient at ease.

---

## PRE-RO ASSESSMENT I

Patient's Name                                      Date
_____

Room Number                    Doctor
_____

Diagnosis:
_____
_____

|  | Correct | Incorrect |
|---|---|---|
| 1. What is your name? | _____ | _____ |
| 2. Where are you living? | _____ | _____ |
| 3. When is your birthday? | _____ | _____ |
| 4. How old are you? | _____ | _____ |
| 5. What year is it now? | _____ | _____ |
| 6. What is the date today? | _____ | _____ |
| 7. What season is it? | _____ | _____ |
| 8. What is the next meal? | _____ | _____ |
| 9. Do you have a roommate? | _____ | _____ |
| 10. What is his/her name? | _____ | _____ |

What do you like best about living here?
_____

Evaluator's comments:
_____
_____
_____

Evaluator                                          Date

---

## 24-HOUR REALITY ORIENTATION

Reality orientation goes on 24 hours a day. Any staff member who notices that a patient or resident seems confused immediately tells the patient where he or she is and why, who the staff member is, and the time of day. The resident is never allowed to retreat into confusion. This information is given first thing in the morning and repeatedly throughout the day. The program is based on consistency and repetition. If even one staff member fails to follow through, the program won't benefit the patients.

*Maintain a calm environment.* A confused patient becomes more confused under tension. Tension may be caused by conflicts with staff members or problems between the patient and the patient's family, for example. Only after the conflicts have been resolved and the environment is calm can the patient be reoriented.

*Keep to a routine so a patient knows what to expect.* Once someone becomes comfortable in a routine, even minor rearrangements of the furniture or daily schedule may cause confusion. If you anticipate any changes in routine, tell the patient about them well ahead of time. As a patient progresses, it can help for him or her to assume the responsibility for part or all of the daily routine, if possible. Letting the person know he or she is expected in the dining room by noon, for example, can give back some independence and increase self-esteem. But make sure the patient is really physically capable.

*Reply clearly and concisely to patient's questions.* Always answer a patient courteously and provide enough details. Likewise, when you ask a patient a question, be clear and allow the individual plenty of time to answer.

*Avoid unnecessarily loud conversation.* Don't raise your voice, and never shout. Loud noises can frighten a geriatric patient and worsen the confusion. Raising your voice does not help a patient who's hard of hearing; all he or she knows is that someone's yelling for no apparent reason. Instead, speak in a firm, confident tone and face the patient. Pronounce words clearly and a little more slowly than normal—don't exaggerate and make faces.

*Give patients clear directions.* A confused man, for example,

107

## PRE-RO ASSESSMENT II

Patient's Name _____ Date _____

Room Number _____ Doctor _____

Diagnosis: _____

_____

_____

1. Can you use the toilet?
   Without help _____
   With assistance _____
   Completely unable _____
   No response _____

2. Can you bathe yourself?
   Without help _____
   With assistance _____
   Completely unable _____
   No response _____

3. Can you dress yourself?
   Without help _____
   With assistance _____
   Completely unable _____
   No response _____

4. Can you feed yourself?
   Without help _____
   With assistance _____
   Completely unable _____
   No response _____

5. Can you brush your hair daily?
   Without help _____
   With assistance _____
   Completely unable _____
   No response _____

6. Do you attend activities here?
   Without help _____

   How often? _____
   With assistance _____
   How often? _____
   Completely unable _____
   No response _____

7. Can you tell the nurses if you need something?
   Without help _____
   With assistance _____
   Completely unable _____
   No response _____

8. Can you write letters and make phone calls?
   Without help _____
   With assistance _____
   Completely unable _____
   No response _____

9. Can you walk freely about?
   Without help _____
   With assistance _____
   Completely unable _____
   No response _____

10. Can you attend a religious service?
    Without help _____
    With assistance _____
    Completely unable _____
    No response _____

Evaluator's comments: _____

_____

_____

_____

Evaluator _____ Date _____

will become more confused if asked to go to his room when he has no idea how to find it. Take the time to give him detailed directions. If necessary, take him there yourself. Color-coded units and rooms are ideal for geriatric patients.

*Encourage correct orientation.* Remind any patient who seems confused of the place, time, day, your name, and even his or her name, if necessary.

*Direct a patient back to reality.* Don't let a patient become more confused. If the patient starts to ramble, help put his or her thoughts in order. Remind the individual to speak slowly and clearly.

*Help the patient understand what you want.* When asking a patient to do an elementary task such as washing his or her face, don't assume anything. Demonstrate the task. Guide the patient's hands through the motions. You may have to do this many times until the task is relearned. A patient, cheerful attitude helps reduce confusion and anxiety.

*Be honest with the patient.* Many times we withold the truth, thinking it will hurt the patient. Being untruthful with a patient, however, only adds to the confusion. If the patient senses you're being untruthful, he or she will become distrustful and difficult to communicate with.

*When you ask a patient to complete a task, act as if you expect it to be done.* First you must decide whether the person is capable of doing what you want. Then, by a positive approach and confident manner, give the patient the impression that he or she can do it. When the task is completed, acknowledge the achievement but don't overpraise it. Too much praise can imply that you had expected failure.

*Be consistent in all your dealings with the patient.* This is the key-stone of the 24-hour RO program. When all staff members use RO consistently, many patients will begin or continue to function with minimal assistance and supervision. This will help make your work easier.

Reality orientation is based on the theory that there's a usable portion of the brain even in severely brain-damaged patients. It is a 24-hour-a-day crusade; the return to reality goes on around the clock. The confused patients are constantly reminded of where they are, why they are there, who you are, and what you expect of them. This basic information, along with the date and time of day, is repeated over and over again. This can easily be accomplished during basic care of such patients. During their baths, meals, activities, and visits with families and friends, make your statements in a conversational tone. Speak slowly, wait for a reply, and make sure your patients can hear and see you well.

In the following example the italicized words are the clues that orient the patient to the surroundings:

Good *morning*, *Mr. MacGonigle*. How are you today? (Wait for a reply.) It's a beautiful *fall day*. It must be *40 degrees* already, and it's such a crisp, clear *morning*. Are you ready for your *breakfast?* (Wait for the patient's reply.) Here's your *breakfast tray*. It's *8 o'clock* in the *morning,* and your *breakfast* is here. These *pancakes* look delicious. *Mr. MacGonigle,* would you like *syrup* on your *pancakes?* (Wait for the patient's reply.)

These few sentences remind the confused patient of the time of day, his name, the season, the weather, and what he's supposed to do (eat breakfast). The three questions give him a sense of responsibility. The pauses for his replies reassure him. Conversations like this, no matter how easy they may seem, must be repeated 24 hours a day, seven days a week.

A federally funded longitudinal study of RO at a large private nursing-home complex, Blue Ridge Haven West in Camp Hill, Pa., supported earlier findings that RO restores memory significantly.[1] A most welcome secondary result of the study was the decided improvement in communication and cooperation among staff members. Most of the employees participated in the preservice and ongoing workshops conducted by the RO certified director of staff education.

## REALITY ORIENTATION CLASSES

More recently, at another Pennsylvania nursing-home facility, Westminster Village in Allentown, the 24-hour RO program is supplemented by regular RO classes for patients, taught by an RO certified director of staff education. Classes for confused patients are held on several levels geared to individual capabilities and progress. Classroom materials usually include individual calendars, word/letter games, blackboards, felt boards, mock-up clocks, building blocks for coordination and color matching, plastic numbers, and large piece puzzles. A prominent visual aid is the RO bulletin board, which lists the name of the facility and its location; the current year, month, and day of the week; the next meal; the weather; and other details (see box). It's placed at eye level. For classes that include both ambulatory and wheelchair patients, two RO boards, at different heights, may be a good idea. At Westminster Village, the RO bulletin board has been kept up to date by an elderly resident who enjoys helping confused patients and, in turn, feels useful.

The same nursing-home complex also starts the day's activities with a 10:00 AM "radio" broadcast over the public-address system (see box). Classes should be limited to five or six people. This gives each patient more time to talk and allows you to give them more individual attention. It is also much easier for a confused person to relate to a small group. The pre-RO assessment tests are an excellent tool for evaluating patients' capabilities and selecting class members.

RO classes should be held daily for one-half hour. Choose a time when the patients are most relaxed and alert, and schedule the class regularly at that hour. Select a quiet, well-lighted, well-ventilated room, preferably with a door that can be shut to eliminate outside stimuli or noise. The room should have a table for patients to sit around and an area where patients in wheelchairs can form a semicircle in front of the instructor and props. The props for RO are inexpensive, ordinary items that can be collected and used on a daily basis:

1. Large clocks
2. Magazines
3. Colorful pictures
4. Posters
5. Maps
6. RO bulletin board(s)
7. Day-by-day calendar
8. Games
9. Record player
10. Radio
11. Picture cards
12. Food models

13.  Flannel or felt boards
14.  Alphabet blocks

The RO bulletin board must be used in basic classes. It can be easily made or inexpensively purchased. A flannel or felt board is ideal. It must be easily legible, with a colored background and large letters.

The three steps in an RO session are (1) establishing a climate of acceptance, (2) building a bridge to reality, and (3) creating a climate of appreciation. Establish a climate of acceptance by first introducing yourself to each patient. Then introduce the patients to each other, one at a time. Don't forget to shake hands; remember the importance of touch. For severely re-

---

## RO RADIO PROGRAM OUTLINE

Good morning. My name is _____ .
This is WWV, the Westminster Village radio station,
on the air Monday thru Friday at 10:00 A.M.
Today is _____, 1987.
The time is 10:00 A.M.
The weather for today is _____
_____

The following people are celebrating birthdays today:
_____
_____

Happy birthday to all of you.

The activities schedule for today is (what, when, where):
_____
_____

A special activity for this week is (what, when, where):
_____

Here are some items in the news today:
_____

This is station WWV signing off until _____ at 10:00 A.M.

---

gressed or withdrawn patients, this first step may be enough.

Start building a bridge to reality by asking each patient to read the RO board. The board may lead spontaneously to a discussion, or you may want to introduce a special topic or ask class members to read and comment on a simple poem. Keep the proceedings as lively and informal as you can. If patients find the class dull and sterile—or worse, threatening to their self-esteem—they won't want to return the next day. Encourage them to chat. If patients start to ramble, steer them back to the subject. Get to know the details of the class members' personal lives. The friendlier the environment, the more cooperative the patients will be in their RO therapy.

| WESTMINSTER VILLAGE ALLENTOWN, PA. |
| --- |
| TODAY IS THURSDAY<br><br>THE DATE IS NOV. 20, 1986<br><br>THE WEATHER IS SUNNY<br><br>THE NEXT HOLIDAY IS THANKSGIVING<br><br>THE NEXT MEAL IS LUNCH<br><br>TOMORROW IS FRIDAY |

The discussion should lead to a climate of appreciation—of self, of each other, or of a poem, for instance. You reinforce this by thanking each group member for attending and by the frequent use of touch.

Before starting each session, make sure all class members are wearing their eyeglasses, hearing aids, dentures, and any other necessary appliances. They can't communicate well if they can't see, hear, or speak clearly. Sit when patients are sitting in order to be at their eye level. Here's a typical, fairly basic RO session:

Instructor: Good morning, everyone. Welcome to your reality orientation class, which meets every day at 10:30 AM. What a beautiful, sunny, crisp morning! Let's begin by reading the reality orientation bulletin board. Mrs. Kline, would you like to read the board first?

Patient Mrs. Kline: This is Westminster Village in Allentown. Today is Thursday, November 20, 1986. The next holiday is Thanksgiving. The next meal is lunch.

Instructor: Thank you, Mrs. Kline. You read the board very well. Does anyone want to tell us what main dish is served on Thanksgiving Day?

Patient Mrs. Brown: Roast turkey and dressing. I really like roast turkey.

Instructor: It's so good, isn't it, Mrs. Brown? What else did you cook at Thanksgiving?

Mrs. Brown: Sweet potatoes, creamed onions, cranberry sauce, and giblet gravy.

Instructor: That all sounds delicious. I bet you're a good cook! How about adding to the menu, Mrs. Jenkins?

Patient Mrs. Jenkins: (No response.)

Instructor: Mrs. Jenkins, can you name some desserts for the class?

Mrs. Jenkins: (No response.)

Instructor: Can someone name a dessert?

Mrs. Kline: Pumpkin pie.

Instructor: Good. Mrs. Jenkins, do you like pumpkin pie?

Mrs. Jenkins: Yes—with ice cream.

Instructor: Excellent, pumpkin pie with ice cream- . . .Now let's get back to the RO board. Mrs. Jenkins, can you read the board for the class?

Mrs. Jenkins: This is Westminster Village in Allentown, Pennsylvania. . .

Instructor: Go on, Mrs. Jenkins.

Mrs. Jenkins: (No response.)

Instructor: I'd like to help you read the RO board. . .Today is Thursday, November 20, 1986. The next holiday is Thanksgiving. The next meal is lunch. . .Can anyone tell us what the temperature is today?

Patient Mr. Davis: It's cold outside.

Instructor: It's very cold. The temperature is 20 degrees. That's unusually cold for November. Mr. Davis, since it's so cold outside, can you tell us what season it will be in a few more weeks?

Mr. Davis: Winter.

Instructor: That's right; winter will be here December 22. Just about a month away. Well, it's 11 o'clock—time for our class to end. Thank you for coming this morning. Let's all shake hands and say goodbye until tomorrow at 10:30.

In addition to a dialogue such as this, the instructor should always identify her/himself and use touch often during the session, especially when praising a participant who gives a correct answer. Move the class along if one member like Mrs. Jenkins doesn't answer or gives an incorrect reply. Never let an unresponsive patient feel you're putting him or her on the spot.

The basic class teaching should continue until the patient is ready to progress to a more advanced experience. You can easily evaluate this by the patient's response to the basic environment. Does the elderly man, for example, know who he is, where he is, who you are, the date, the time? Is he reaching out to other residents and members of the class? The time given to an RO patient is as long as he or she needs. Don't hury him; be patient. RO is usually a long, slow process. The basic RO classes can take as little as a week for one person and as long as three or four months for another.

For some, RO may not work at all. Dr. James C. Folsom, who pioneered the development of the theory and techniques, states: "Reality Orientation does not work all the time, nor at the same speed, nor to the same degree for every patient. Each patient is different."[2] But, since stopping regression is also considered success in an RO program, it's important not to get discouraged.

More advanced RO classes are similar to the basic session.

The advanced class meets daily at a regular time for 30 minutes. The RO board is reviewed in a more conversational tone, and a higher performance level is expected. Simple crafts can be started and group activities with classmates initiated. The advanced class should be more individualized. The purpose and procedures are the same for the advanced class as for the basic class. Emphasis should still be placed on time, place, and person. The principal props should still be used regularly for continued review and reality orientation.

## GUIDELINES FOR CONDUCTING AN RO CLASS

1. The RO instructor or a resident should prepare the RO board and make sure it's up to date and accurate. The classroom should be well lighted and ventilated.
2. Make sure patients are wearing their eyeglasses, hearing aids, dentures, and any other necessary appliances. Sit at eye level.
3. Begin the class by introducing yourself to each patient. Always call the patient by his or her name and encourage him or her to call others in the class by their names. Shake hands with each one of the patients and encourage all patients to shake hands with each other.
4. Introduce the class: "This is a class designed to help us remember and to exercise our minds. Class will meet every day for one-half hour at _____."
5. Have each patient read the board. After he or she successfully reads the information on the board, get him or her talking about him or herself, their family , hometown, or former occupation. Be prepared to know all this information so you can recognize mistakes and encourage correct responses.
6. A large mock-up clock may be used in conjunction with a real clock. Set the mock-up clock at the time of the class and ask a patient to read it.
7. Remember that the attention span of these patients is limited. If someone is unresponsive or answers an elementary question incorrectly, make him aware that you appreciate their effort and give them a few clues. But don't drag it out to the point where the other patients get bored or the

116

## RO PROGRESS REPORT (CONTINUED)

Resident's Name _____ Group Number _____

Leader(s) _____ Date _____

|  | 1st | 4th | 8th | 12th |  |
|---|---|---|---|---|---|
| **READING** |  |  |  |  |  |
|  | ____ | ____ | ____ | ____ | Refuses to read |
|  | ____ | ____ | ____ | ____ | Cannot see to read |
|  | ____ | ____ | ____ | ____ | Participates |
| **GROUP RELATIONS** |  |  |  |  |  |
|  | ____ | ____ | ____ | ____ | Participates in inter-group comments |
|  | ____ | ____ | ____ | ____ | Has good relationship with others in group |
|  | ____ | ____ | ____ | ____ | Does not resent being interrupted |
|  | ____ | ____ | ____ | ____ | Resents being interrupted |
|  | ____ | ____ | ____ | ____ | Shy |
|  | ____ | ____ | ____ | ____ | Interrupts others |
|  | ____ | ____ | ____ | ____ | Argues with others |
|  | ____ | ____ | ____ | ____ | Gets angry easily |

ENJOYMENT  YES ____ SOMETIMES ____ NO ____ Does resident seem to enjoy meetings?

PROGRESS  YES ____ NO ____ Since the last report, if any, has resident shown any improvement in meeting? If yes, in what way?

YES ____ NO ____ Since the last report, if any, has resident shown any improvement on the ward?

PLACEMENT

_____ Do you think resident should stay with the same group?

_____ Move to a lower group?

_____ Move to an advanced group?

# R O  PROGRESS REPORT

Resident's Name _____  Group Number _____

Leader(s) _____  Date _____

| | 1st | 4th | 8th | 12th | Week |
|---|---|---|---|---|---|
| **INTEREST** | | | | | |
| | ____ | ____ | ____ | ____ | Refuses to come to meeting |
| | ____ | ____ | ____ | ____ | Attends but shows little interest |
| | ____ | ____ | ____ | ____ | Shows some interest |
| | ____ | ____ | ____ | ____ | Interested |
| **AWARENESS** | | | | | |
| | ____ | ____ | ____ | ____ | Usually unaware of what is going on |
| | ____ | ____ | ____ | ____ | Distracted by voices |
| | ____ | ____ | ____ | ____ | Sometimes unaware of what is going on |
| | ____ | ____ | ____ | ____ | Usually aware of proceedings |
| | ____ | ____ | ____ | ____ | Always aware of proceedings |
| **PARTICIPATION** | | | | | |
| | ____ | ____ | ____ | ____ | Does not talk |
| | ____ | ____ | ____ | ____ | Sometimes answers direct questions |
| | ____ | ____ | ____ | ____ | Usually answers direct questions |
| | ____ | ____ | ____ | ____ | Sometimes volunteers comments |
| **KNOWLEDGE** | | | | | |
| | ____ | ____ | ____ | ____ | Has very little knowledge of average topic |
| | ____ | ____ | ____ | ____ | Occasionally answers incorrectly or not on topic |
| | ____ | ____ | ____ | ____ | Has good knowledge of average topic |

*continued*

unresponsive patient feels you're putting pressure on him.

8. Generate stimulating conversation. Here are some simple questions you might ask during a basic RO class:
   What season is this?
   What kind of animal barks, moos, baas?
   What did you have for breakfast today?
   What color is the opposite of black?
   What's your favorite holiday?

9. Establish attainable goals and give reward, praise, and recognition immediately. Face the patient when speaking and touch them when appropriate.

10. Have a disruptive patient removed if he starts to disturb the other class members.

## WRITTEN RECORDS

It isn't always necessary to keep written records of patients' progress in an RO program. However, progress reports can be very useful in deciding whether to hospitalize a nursing-home

---

**RO LOG**

Class Number _____

Date Started        Date Ended _____

Leader(s) _____

| Date | Topics, Activities | Residents Attending (Initials) |
|------|--------------------|--------------------------------|
|      |                    |                                |
|      |                    |                                |
|      |                    |                                |
|      |                    |                                |
|      |                    |                                |

Comments: _____

---

resident, release a patient to their family or halfway house, or transfer a patient to another group. Written reports can also help a nursing-home director or geriatric-care supervisor in reporting to the members of a patient's family. Finally, written reports make it possible to evaluate the effectiveness of an RO group and its leader.

Progress reports should be made at the end of the first, fourth, eighth, and 12th weeks of the program. If the series of classes is scheduled to end or break after 12 weeks, members of the group should be informed well in advance; after all, that's part of the reality they need to accept. If the series is planned to run continuously, a fresh form can be used for the 16th, 20th, 24th, and 28th weeks, and so on.

It's also helpful to keep an RO log that shows the number of residents who attended each day, the discussion topics or activities, and the instructor's comments. Was there a noticeable drop in attendence the day after a certain topic was discussed or a particular activity carried out? If so, the session may have bored, offended, or threatened some patients; better substitute another activity in your future RO program plans.

---

**References**
1. Kohut JJ: Unpublished observations, 1977-1986.
2. Folsom JC: "Major Problems in the Treatment of 'Senility'." Paper presented at the 18th Annual Conference of the Veterans Administration: Studies in Mental Health and Behavioral Sciences, Washington, D.C., March 28-30, 1973.

**Resources**
Bennett R: *Aging: Isolation and Resocialization.* New York, Van Nostrand Reinhold, 1980.
    Describes practical programs that reduce isolation among both the community-based aged and residents of geriatric insitutions.
Sprott RL: *Age, Learning Ability, and Intelligence.* New York, Van Nostrand Reinhold, 1980.

# 13

# REMOTIVATION THERAPY AND OTHER MODALITIES

Remotivation therapy is similar to reality orientation and incorporates many aspects of RO. But there are important differences.

Whereas RO is used primarily to help confused geriatric or chronic brain syndrome (CBS) patients adjust to their surroundings, remotivation is directed more toward withdrawn but still verbal individuals who need stimulation to participate in their environment. Remotivation therapy is an objective technique used with groups, designed to reach the unwounded areas of the patient's personality and help him want to "live again." The technique was originated by a volunteer in a Veterans Administration hospital. It has gained such wide acceptance that standard courses in it are now taught by certified remotivation trainers who are members of the National Remotivation Technique Organization (NRTO).

A patient in a nursing home, rehabilitation facility, or mental institution may have access to several kinds of treatment, including occupational work, rehabilitation, drug, art, music, physical, medical, and psychiatric therapy. Unless he willingly participates in these programs, the full therapeutic benefit of the therapy won't be realized. Remotivation therapy provides the extra "push" that can help him participate. With some exceptions, it can be used regardless of the patient's age, illness, or length of institutionalization.

A trained aide or leader meets once or twice a week for about an hour with a small group of patients—no more than 12. The patients are encouraged, not required, to attend regularly. The leader brings up an objective topic for discussion—current events, natural history, sports, cars, for instance. The leader plans the material according to five specific steps in the remotivation process:

1. Creating a climate of acceptance.
2. Using objective ideas to build a bridge to the real world.
3. Sharing the world in which we live.
4. Appreciating the work of the world.
5. Creating a climate of appreciation.

The discussion topic can come from almost any objective— i.e., nonemotional—area of common interest. Choose material you think will interest your patients and that is also familiar to you. Present it at a level the patients can deal with. The discussion topic should be as specific as possible: Instead of the general sport of baseball, get the patients talking about yesterday's game if you know they watched it; instead of "Do you like poetry?" read a short, simple poem or—better—ask one of the group members to do so. Start positively and keep the discussion lively. Bounce simple questions around the group; try to get each patient to answer at least once. Avoid personality clashes among group members, and don't let one or two patients monopolize the discussion.

## PROCEDURE

Arrange chairs, including your own, in a circle. Let the patients sit wherever they want in the circle. Start on time and try to keep to the following schedule:

*Step 1: Climate of acceptance* (5 minutes). Greet patients by name and shake hands. Make any necessary introductions. Get the members to relax with small talk, compliments, and so on.

*Step 2: Bridge to the real world* (10 to 15 minutes.) Bounce questions around the group to warm the members up. Ask questions without right or wrong answers—for example, Where would you like to be? What's your favorite color? Pose only one question at a time. If you can, make the last question lead into the poem or other short passage you've chosen. The poem, in turn, should lead into the main discussion topic.

*Step 3: The world we live in* (10 to 15 minutes.) Use pictures, short articles, slides, or other props to make the topic vivid. Your questions should follow the journalist's *Who? What? How? Where? When?* The objective is to encourage the patients to talk and share their ideas and experiences. Accept whatever the patient has to offer unless it's abusive or off the track. Don't interrupt except to steer a wandering patient back to the topic. Remember: People enjoy talking more than listening.

*Step 4: The work of the world* (10 to 15 minutes.) How does the discussion topic relate to people's daily lives? How do they carry out their jobs? What do they need to know in order to do their work? Would any of the patients in your group like to do this kind of work?

*Step 5: Climate of appreciation* (5 to 10 minutes.) As you thank each patient for attending the session, try to get his or her reaction to the discussion. If they didn't say much during the session, you can ask them why. Let them know you'd like to hear anything they have to say. As you bid each patient good-bye, remind them of the date of the next session and tell them you look forward to seeing them.

## BENEFITS OF REMOTIVATION THERAPY

Remotivation sessions have three important benefits for the patient. (1) They stimulate the mind and help bring them out of the shell into which they've retreated. (2) By actively soliciting interest in an objective, "real-world" subject, they help the patient put personal problems in perspective and keep him or her in touch with life outside the institution. People in institutions tend to become passive and dependent. Focusing on the real world helps remind them that it's possible and desirable for individuals to take responsibility for their lives, to live freely, and contribute actively to society. (3) Remotivation therapy gives patients practice in interacting with others in an atmosphere of acceptance and friendship. Because a "normal" person—the group leader—encourages their participation, self-esteem is increased.

The hospital or nursing-home personnel who lead remotivation groups benefit from this experience by increasing their understanding of patients and their problems. Every patient is a person, not just a set of symptoms or a peculiar behavior pattern—a fact that even the most experienced and compassionate nurse or aide can occasionally forget. Bringing an emotionally disturbed person out into the real world, helping him to grow and healing emotional wounds, is a deeply gratifying experience.

Remotivation groups also help the psychiatric staff. A well-trained leader can do some of the doctor's spadework by stimulating the patients' desire for recovery. The leader's written notes can provide the doctor with valuable clues about patients' vocational and other objective interests.

## WRITTEN RECORDS

Paper work is a must. Because the ultimate goal of remotivation therapy is to get the patient out of the institution and functioning constructively as an independent individual, it's vital to keep written records of progress. The kinds of records vary from institution to institution, but they include individual progress reports and your own log, like the records recommended for reality orientation groups.

## WHO CAN BE A GROUP LEADER?

The most important qualification is your own personal interest in helping patients. A warm, understanding attitude, resourcefulness in dealing with unexpected situations (whether a patient suddenly becomes abusive or whether you've just run out of prepared discussion topics, you must be in control of the situation at all times), and willingness to give more than you think you've got are crucial to the program's success. The other vital factor is the approval of the director and nursing supervisor of the facility.

The remotivation program in each facility is under the charge of a coordinator. He or she cooperates with the director and nursing supervisor in selecting trainees and arranging for their instruction, keeps a file of records on the program, helps schedule group sessions, establishes a library of materials for use in the remotivation groups, and acts as spokesperson for the program.

All personnel should receive general orientation in remotivation therapy. As in 24-hour RO, everyone's cooperation is needed for the program to succeed. One slighting remark or careless treatment from an unthinking staff member can undo weeks of effort.

Anyone who wishes to become a remotivation group leader must first take a 30-hour basic remotivation course taught by a certified instructor. The course may be taken inhouse, if a certified instructor is available there, or at a regional training center. The course's content may be tailored to the facility (nursing home, mental hospital, or halfway house, for example), but must be consistent with the standards of the National Remotivation Technique Organization, Inc. (NRTO).

Following the basic course is a series of 24 group sessions with patients. A certificate is awarded after the first 12 sessions, and a remotivation pin is given to those who complete all 24.

The aspiring group leader must then take a 30-hour advanced remotivation course, followed by another 24 sessions with patient groups. On completion of these requirements, a certificate is awarded, qualifying the recipient to act as a certified group leader.

A group leader may go on to become an instructor by taking a 30-hour instructors training course and satisfying other requirements. A certified instructor is qualified to set up a regional training center at the institution where he or she is employed.

The NRTO publishes a Remotivation Information Kit ($3.00 each; plus postage). Specify Nursing Home or Psychiatric Edition when ordering. The NRTO will also provide, on request, the addresses of facilities in any region of the United States that offer workshops and certificates in remotivation therapy. Information can be obtained from:

National Remotivation Technique Organization, Inc.
Ms. Ruth V. Traylor, Director
National Headquarters
Pilgrim Psychiatric Center
P.O. Box 1096

West Brentwood, NY 11717
(516) 434-5094

## OCCUPATIONAL THERAPY

Paramedical specialties like occupational therapy are included under most Medicare programs. The American Occupational Therapy Association (AOTA) is the national organization primarily involved in advocacy roles for occupational therapy throughout the United States. Occupational therapy is defined by AOTA as "the art and science of directing man's participation in a selected activity to restore, reinforce, and enhance performance, facilitate learning of those skills and functions essential for adaptation and productivity, diminish or correct pathology and to promote and maintain good health."[1]

The occupational therapists can have a key role in any program designed to help the elderly. The therapist possesses the skills to assess the interests and capabilities of the client or patient and to channel the person's energy and leisure-time activities in more meaningful and enjoyable ways.

## ART THERAPY

Compared to the other "therapy" professions, art therapy is the new kid on the block, but it is no less important than any other more well-known specialties. The American Art Therapy Association (AATA) is the national advocacy agency for art therapy. It provides information and ideas via its publications, meetings, and seminars. Art therapy, like so many super-specialities, is hard to define. Basically, it is described as the use of visual art to assist integration or reintegration of personality as applied in education, rehabilitation, and psychotherapy. The art therapist is an artist, teacher, and therapist. Art therapy is much more than patients sitting around making pictures or molding clay and then chatting with a trained therapist about their work and its symbolism.

With institutionalized elderly, the therapist attempts to make available to the patients the pleasures and satisfaction that creative work can provide, and with the therapist's insights and therapeutic skills, make such experiences meaningful and valuable.

The AATA warns all health-care agencies and nursing-home programs to be cautious about employing or enlisting the services of any kind of therapist, not just art therapists, unless they have proper credentials and are properly registered or licensed. There are many fine art educators but too few qualified art therapists. Volunteer "do-gooders" who purport to be qualified can do more harm than good to patients.

## MUSIC THERAPY

Music therapy is the use of music along with therapeutic procedures to help persons address emotional, physical, and mental conditions, and assist them in adjusting to stressful life situations.

Therapeutic applications of music vary. The choice of music and the method of participation (active, passive, creative) depends upon the preference and experiences of the patient. Music can be live or recorded, vocal or instrumental, familiar or unfamiliar, old standards or newly created tunes. Singing with or being sung to by another person offers an entirely different emotional and physical experience from playing an instrument, listening to an instrument, or listening to various kinds of recordings. Music can be a solitary or a group experience.

The presence of music can reduce reactions to pain during treatments throughout an illness by providing a diversion or a focus of interest, by offering some sense of control of the setting, and by promoting muscle relaxation. Through the study of words of songs, known as lyric interpretation, the therapist can help a patient who may not be able to express fear, anger, and other emotions. With the assistance of the therapist, the patient is able to express feelings through the lyrics using the third person, such as singing about not having a friend when the going gets tough. The therapist is trained in the selecting of music in which the music alone or both the text and the music are likely to promote disclosure of suppressed feelings by the patient who finds expression difficult.

In determining the best kind of therapy, the therapist must consider the role of music in the patient's life. Music is a universal human behavior found in all cultures and at all stages of development and life. Music is processed directly by the brain and thus needs no decoding or interpretation. It elicits both voluntary and involuntary physiological responses, and, through association, promotes recollection of significant persons, events, and places. Music can be a powerful group experience by providing a setting for acceptable shared feelings, a sense of self-control, and important aesthetic expressions.

The National Association of Music Therapy (NAMT) provides information to nursing homes interested in establishing music therapy programs. The NAMT's headquarters may be contacted:

National Association of Music Therapy
1133 15th Street, N.W.
Suite 1000
Washington, D.C. 20005
(202) 429-9440

## REMINISCENCE

Disc jockeys on local radio stations often play "oldies but goodies" records.

We all enjoy reminiscing about past pleasures and experiences. It makes us feel good. A favorite tune often reminds us of a particular special friend or event. Happiness can be defined for my elderly persons as recollections of warm and meaningful memories. Talking about past experiences is an excellent therapeutic technique because reminiscence is a primary cognitive characteristic of the geriatric stage of life.

Establishing reminiscing groups in board and care homes or long-term facilities like nursing homes can be an extremely positive activity. The multidisciplinary team should be used whenever possible in implementing different rehabilitation programs; this is especially important in reminiscing therapy.

Reminiscing therapy helps increase self-esteem, sensory stimulation, and general socialization skills, and reinforces friendship networks. Reality orientation is a structured dimension of reminiscence for the confused patient.

Group reminiscing in nursing homes is a way of sharing memories with others who have experienced the same historical events and time span of life. The life review process is characterized by a progressive return to days past and an "evaluation" of the worth of life. In a manner of speaking, the patient is taking a final look at his or her life from a new perspective. This preoccupation is activated by an awareness of approaching death. The patient is attempting to recall and reconcile past successes and failures. For the institutionalized elderly, the formal involvement of qualified staff in this life review is important.

---

**References**
1. *Occupational Therapy: Its Definition and Functions.* Rockville, MD, American Occupational Association, 1969.

# 14

# GOAL PLANNING

Goal planning is a method of helping someone improve performance. For a patient or resident in a nursing home or hospital, the ultimate goal is to live as independently as possible within physical limitations.

An elderly person can still be a whole person. He or she has the need to grow and change; he can still thrive on challenge. His innate human dignity causes resentment of the dependence and passivity that come from playing by the institution's rules—the institutionalization syndrome described in Chapter 8.

Goal planning must actively involve the individual patient or resident. He must cooperate; you can't do it all for him. Therefore, the first step is to help him list his personal strengths and needs.

- Strengths can include what the individual enjoys doing, what he does without being reminded, what he does well, whom he likes and trusts, what he likes (physical, social, spiritual, intellectual activities), and what his achievements have been.
- Needs might be these: to become more independent and self-sufficient, to become more active physically, to exercise his or her mind by taking up a hobby or other interest, or to become more active socially.

Write his needs positively—for example, "needs to make more friends," not "doesn't have any friends." The list of strengths should be longer than the list of needs. It's important not to discourage the patient by letting the list of needs get too long; keep it to three items at most.

The second step is to help the patient plan the methods he'll use to satisfy his needs. Help him state them concretely and positively. For instance, if he's had a mild stroke and has trouble writing but needs to keep in closer touch with his children who live out of state, he'll need physical therapy to help him regain the ability to write letters. Or if he needs to make more friends, he will do so by spending more time in the lounge or solarium and by actively introducing himself to other residents.

Set realistic target dates and distinguish between short- and long-term goals. As in the preceding examples, the patient's short-term goal would be to begin physical therapy by the beginning of the next week. The physical therapist or rehabilitation specialist may then be able to give him a realistic idea of when he'll be able to write again and achieve his long term goal of keeping in closer touch with his children. Similarly, the patient's short-term goal could be to become acquainted with one new person every day for a week; his long-term goal of making more friends would be achieved almost automatically as he spent more time with people he found most compatible.

In order to achieve his goals, the patient must have the help of the staff members. Spell out the responsibilities of all concerned and give them copies of the patient's goal plan.

Patient plan-of-care conferences should be conducted on a weekly basis with both professional and nonprofessional support staff participating. At least every few months, members of the patient's family should be encouraged to attend and contribute at the conference. This is especially important for confused patients or when there is a drastic change in the patient's condition. Each professional staffer, representing a different discipline, should develop a method by which the patient can accomplish or at least make progress toward accomplishing goals.

Finally, review the plan periodically with the patient. As

one goal is achieved, another can be substituted. In this way, the patient is constantly challenged to grow, change, and keep from sinking into an institutional rut.

# APPENDICES

# APPENDIX 1 '

## A CONCEPT OF IN-SERVICE EDUCATION
## IN NURSING HOMES

*Definition.* In-service education in nursing homes is a systematic and continuing process of providing job-related learning experiences for all personnel responsible for direct and indirect care and services to patients/residents.

*Philosophy.* The ultimate goal of in-service education in nursing homes is to improve the quality of life among patients/residents. Therefore a philosophy of in-service education in nursing homes reflects a commitment to the following principles:

- All personnel must be offered the opportunity for growth, development, advancement of knowledge, understanding, and skills to help them improve their on-the-job performance; in-service education provides such opportunities.
- In-service education enables personnel to provide care and services that promote and maintain independent functioning among patients/residents.
- Continued improvement of the quality of in-service education serves the best interests of the nursing home, its personnel, and patients/residents.
- Continued improvement of in-service education requires the active participation of representatives of all levels of personnel responsible for direct and indirect nursing-home care and services.
- In-service education is an integral part of the management process; the quality of its practice is determined by the climate of acceptance, appreciation, and support engendered by attitudes and actions of administrative and supervisory personnel at all levels of nursing-home organization.
- The climate of acceptance and appreciation of the values of in-service education is established through such administrative action as (1) allocating money, time, and other resources to the in-service education program and (2) encouraging all personnel to communicate their ideas and information about in-service education goals and processes.

*Components.* In-service education encompasses the following four major components:

1. Orientation—to the home's specific objectives, organization, personnel policies, job descriptions, and physical plant in which care and services are provided to patients/residents. This includes ongoing orientation of all personnel to any changes in the nursing home.

2. Skill training—to develop competence related to physical needs of patients/residents, e.g., nursing care, food service, activities of daily living, safety, and application of written procedures for care of persons with acute or chronic illnesses, including rehabilitative and restorative techniques.

3. Continuing education—to build additional competence and integrate interpersonal skills into all aspects of interaction with patients/residents, families, other visitors to the home, personnel from other departments within the home, etc. Continuing education provides new knowledge, understanding, and skills based on findings of research in the physical and behavioral sciences, e.g., new techniques for serving physical, social, emotional, and spiritual needs of aging persons with illnesses or disabilities in institutional settings.

4. Leadership and management development—for selected personnel who show potential for learning and applying new methods of leadership and management; remedial training for personnel in leadership and management positions who show evidence of need for assistance in this area of on-the-job performance.

*Process.* The in-service education process applies principles of adult education and motivation by:

- Involving trainees in planning and conducting their own learning experiences;
- Building on and making appropriate use of trainees' previous experience and relating this experience to new ways of doing things;
- Providing immediate opportunities to apply new learning to the solution of practical problems; actively involving trainees in evaluating the results of their exposure to the in-service education program.

It is a systematic process that involves application of the following steps:

- Formulating statements of general and specific objectives;
- Gathering information relevant to needs, problems, and objectives; identifying resources that can be useful in serving needs, solving problems, and achieving specific objectives;
- Planning and implementing the program, e.g., scheduling in-service education sessions, using written program plans and lesson plans;
- Evaluating results of the program; modifying it as necessary to serve changing needs, to solve new or unresolved problems, and to achieve original and additional objectives.

*Benefits.* For the staff, in-service education:
- Promotes understanding and commitment to the goals of the home through orientation programming;
- Provides satisfaction by developing the skills needed to do a good job on a continuing basis;
- Offers additional satisfaction of the universal human desire for growth and development by providing refresher information and training in new skills;
- Gives staff members a chance to grow with their jobs and to take on additional responsibilities, by offering courses in leadership and management development;
- Actively involves staff members in checking on their own levels of performance and in setting higher standards of on-the-job performance;
- Promotes mutual respect for each other's work roles and responsibilities by giving personnel from various disciplines opportunities to exchange ideas and information and to solve problems together.

For the home, in-service education can promote a higher level of patient/resident care and develop a more efficient and loyal staff. The benefits derived from these achievements may include the following:
- An improved public image of the home within the immediate community (and of nursing homes in general);
- A new perception of the nursing home as a laboratory for ana-

lyzing problems and working out practical solutions to the problems of delivering care and services to chronically ill, aging patients/residents;

- The development of a "neutral" environment in which interpersonal and interdepartmental disagreements can be resolved; where it is a problem, staff turnover can be reduced.

*Conclusion.* In-service education is instrumental in developing human resources needed to provide care and services that satisfy the complex needs of personnel, patients/residents, families, and the community in which a home is located. In-service education is a continuing responsibility shared by administrative and other personnel responsible for the safety and well-being of nursing-home patients/residents.

---

Adapted, with permission, from Nursing Home Trainer Program NYM/RMP Project No. 20 61-70 A, United Hospital Fund of New York, December 1972. This concept of in-service education in nursing homes was developed by participants and staff of the Nursing Home Trainer Program, a demonstration project conducted by the United Hospital Fund of New York and funded by a grant from the New York Metropolitan/Regional Medical Program.

# APPENDIX 2

## HUMAN NEEDS

All people—no matter who they are, where they live, or how old they are—have certain needs. How are these needs met in your own life, and how are they met in a nursing home? What important differences do you see, and how would they affect you if you were suddenly placed in a nursing home? Discuss these questions in groups of three or four to give each person a chance to speak.

1. Physiological needs
   a. Hunger
   b. Thirst
   c. Elimination
   d. Health care
   e. Cleanliness
   f. Others
2. Needs related to shelter
   a. Protection from weather
   b. Privacy
   c. Predictable environment
   d. Comfort
   e. Protection of possessions
   f. Access to amenities (telephone, television, etc.)
   g. Access to outdoors
   h. Others
3. Need for love and affection. Each group member should take turns pretending to be paralyzed from the neck down and unable to speak. Her partner should feed her.
   a. What physical boundaries around ourselves do we create under normal social conditions?
   b. Do these boundaries change if we become helpless?
   c. Can drawing back our boundaries express love? How?
   d. Is expression of love and affection proper and beneficial in an institutional setting? When?
4. Sexual needs
   a. Opportunities
   b. Manifestations

    c. Variations among individuals
    d. Attitudes of other people
    e. Is the shoe on the other foot with sexually active elderly people—i.e., are they viewed as rebels and nonconformists, and does this upset us?

5. Social needs
    a. Communication
    b. Sharing
    c. Need to feel needed
    d. Variations among individuals

6. Ego needs
    a. Sense of achievement
    b. Self-esteem
    c. Freedom to risk failure
    d. Others

7. Self-actualization
    a. Personal growth
    b. Making the most of individual talents
    c. Overcoming handicaps
    d. Others

# APPENDIX 3

## EMPATHY TRAINING

These exercises in empathy training—learning to feel as others do—are meant to be carried out in partnerships within a group. Members should take turns participating in each exercise so that everyone gets a chance to do and be done unto. Everyone should also get a chance to express her reactions to these experiences of sensory, motor, and social deprivation.

### SENSORY LOSS

Find out what it's like—

- To have poor sight: cover a pair of eyeglasses with clear plastic wrap and try to read a newspaper.
- To be hard of hearing: stuff cotton in your ears and listen to a radio or someone speaking on the telephone.
- To be arthritic: tape the second knuckles of your hands loosely together and/or tape a ruler to the side of your leg above and below the knee; then try to button a shirt and/or climb stairs.
- To have lost your sense of smell: stuff cotton in your nostrils and eat an apple.
- To have trouble speaking because of stroke or dental problems: repeat the Pledge of Allegiance at normal speed with a hard candy ball in your mouth.
- To have shaky hands: write your name with your nondominant hand.

### MOTOR LOSS

These exercises emphasize the elderly patient's dependence on those who care for him.

1. Sit in a wheelchair and chat with other group members. One member or the instructor should abruptly wheel you away in the middle of the conversation, without excusing herself or apologizing.
2. Lie propped up in bed and have your partner feed you a little faster than you can comfortably chew and swallow food or drink.

3. Lie in bed and have your partner tie your hand to the side. Wait alone in the room, with the door closed, until she decides to return.

## QUESTIONS FOR GROUP DISCUSSION

1. What were your feelings about yourself during these empathy-training exercises?
2. Did your partner's behavior change? If so, how?
3. Did your attitude toward your partner change? If so, in what way or ways?
4. Did your partner's attitude toward you change? If so, in what way or ways?
5. What can you do to make life more pleasant and comfortable for persons with such handicaps?

- For poor sight: provide good, direct lighting; make sure eyeglasses are clean.
- For hearing loss: make sure hearing aid is in place and working properly; speak clearly, slowly, and directly.
- For stiff joints: help only as much as the patient needs; touch and handle his body gently and tenderly.
- For loss of senses of smell and taste: make sure food is warm, appetizing, and attractively served; make sure dentures are in place and clean; allow a hand-fed patient plenty of time to chew and swallow.
- For slowness in action and response: allow plenty of time; never rush a patient.
- Help patients keep themselves neat, clean, and becomingly dressed; shave men if necessary, and remove facial hair from women; remember mouth, hand, and foot care; encourage patients to wear clean clothes and use deodorant.
- Use reality orientation techniques (Chapter 12) if a patient seems confused.

# APPENDIX 4

## HELPFUL HINTS TO FRIENDS OF
## HARD-OF-HEARING PEOPLE

When talking to the hard-of-hearing person you will be able to help him understand you more clearly if you follow these simple suggestions:

1. Talk at a moderate rate.
2. Keep your voice at about the same volume throughout, without dropping the voice at the end of each sentence.
3. Always speak as clearly and accurately as possible. Consonants, especially, should be articulated with care.
4. Do not "over-articulate"; i.e., mouthing or overdoing articulation is just as bad as mumbling.
5. Pronounce every name with care. Make a reference to the name for easier understanding, as: Joan, "the girl from the office," or Penney's, "the downtown store."
6. Change to a new subject at a slower rate, making sure that the person follows the change. A key word or two at the beginning of a new topic is a good indicator.
7. Do not attempt to converse while you have something in your mouth, such as a pipe, cigar, cigarette, or chewing gum. Do not cover your mouth with your hand.
8. Talk in a normal tone of voice. Shouting does not make your voice more distinct. In some instances shouting makes it more difficult for a hard-of-hearing person to understand.
9. Address the listener directly. Do not turn away in the middle of a remark or story. Make sure that the listener can see your face easily and that a good light is on it.
10. Use longer phrases, which tend to be easier to understand than short ones. For example, "Will you get me a drink of water?" presents much less difficulty than "Will you get me a drink?" Word choice is important here. Fifteen and fifty cents may be confused, but a half dollar is clearer.

Courtesy of the Sacramento Hearing Society, Inc.

# APPENDIX 5

## A PATIENT'S BILL OF RIGHTS

The American Hospital Association presents a Patient's Bill of Rights with the expectation that observance of these rights will contribute to more effective patient care and greater satisfaction for the patient, his physician, and the hospital organization. Further, the Association presents these rights in the expectation that they will be supported by the hospital on behalf of its patients, as an integral part of the healing process. It is recognized that a personal relationship between the physician and the patient is essential for the provision of proper medical care. The traditional physician-patient relationship takes on a new dimension when care is rendered within an organizational structure. Legal precedent has established that the institution itself also has a responsibility to the patient. It is in recognition of these factors that these rights are affirmed.

1. The patient has the right to considerate and respectful care.
2. The patient has the right to obtain from his physician complete current information concerning his diagnosis, treatment, and prognosis in terms the patient can understand. When it is not medically advisable to give such information to the patient, the information should be made available to an appropriate person in his behalf. He has the right to know, by name, the physician responsible for coordinating his care.
3. The patient has the right to receive from his physician information necessary to give informed consent prior to the start of any procedure and/or treatment. Except in emergencies, such information for informed consent should include but not necessarily be limited to the specific procedure and/or treatment, the medically significant risks involved, and the probable duration of incapacitation. Where medically significant alternatives for care or treatment exist, or when the patient requests information concerning medical alternatives, the patient has the right to such information. The patient also has the right to know the name of the person responsible for the procedures and/or treatment.

4. The patient has the right to refuse treatment to the extent permitted by law and to be informed of the medical consequences of his action.
5. The patient has the right to every consideration of his privacy concerning his own medical care program. Case discussion, consultation, examination, and treatment are confidential and should be conducted discreetly. Those not directly involved in his care must have the permission of the patient to be present.
6. The patient has the right to expect that all communications and records pertaining to his care should be treated as confidential.
7. The patient has the right to expect that within its capacity a hospital must make reasonable response to the request of a patient for services. The hospital must provide evaluation, service, and/or referral as indicated by the urgency of the case. When medically permissible, a patient may be transferred to another facility only after he has received complete information concerning the needs for and alternatives to such a transfer. The institution to which the patient is to be transferred must first have accepted the patient for transfer.
8. The patient has the right to obtain information as to any relationship of his hospital to other health care and educational institutions insofar as his care is concerned. The patient has the right to obtain information as to the existence of any professional relationships among individuals, by name, who are treating him.
9. The patient has the right to be advised if the hospital proposes to engage in or perform human experimentation affecting his care or treatment. The patient has the right to refuse to participate in such research projects.
10. The patient has the right to expect reasonable continuity of care. He has the right to know in advance what appointment times and physicians are available and where. The patient has the right to expect that the hospital will provide a mechanism whereby he is informed by his physician or a delegate of the physician of the patient's continuing health care requirements following discharge.

11. The patient has the right to examine and receive an explanation of his bill regardless of source of payment.
12. The patient has the right to know what hospital rules and regulations apply to his conduct as a patient.

No catalog of rights can guarantee for the patient the kind of treatment he has a right to expect. A hospital has many functions to perform, including the prevention and treatment of disease, the education of both health professionals and patients, and the conduct of clinical research. All these activities must be conducted with an overriding concern for the patient, and, above all, the recognition of his dignity as a human being. Success in achieving this recognition assures success in the defense of the rights of the patient.

---